Adventure Sports

An Introduction to Adventure Racing

(A Beginner's Guide to Making Money as an Adventure Sports)

David Hendon

Published By **Zoe Lawson**

David Hendon

All Rights Reserved

Adventure Sports: An Introduction to Adventure Racing (A Beginner's Guide to Making Money as an Adventure Sports)

ISBN 978-1-77485-720-5

No part of this guidebook shall be reproduced in any form without permission in writing from the publisher except in the case of brief quotations embodied in critical articles or reviews.

Legal & Disclaimer

The information contained in this ebook is not designed to replace or take the place of any form of medicine or professional medical advice. The information in this ebook has been provided for educational & entertainment purposes only.

The information contained in this book has been compiled from sources deemed reliable, and it is accurate to the best of the Author's knowledge; however, the Author cannot guarantee its accuracy and validity and cannot be held liable for any errors or omissions. Changes are periodically made to this book. You must consult your doctor or get professional medical advice before using any of the suggested remedies, techniques, or information in this book.

Upon using the information contained in this book, you agree to hold harmless the Author from and against any damages, costs, and expenses, including any legal fees potentially resulting from the application of any of the information provided by this guide. This disclaimer applies to any damages or injury caused by the use and application, whether directly or indirectly, of any advice or information presented, whether for breach of contract, tort, negligence, personal injury, criminal intent, or under any other cause of action.

You agree to accept all risks of using the information presented inside this book. You need to consult a professional medical practitioner in order to ensure you are both able and healthy enough to participate in this program.

TABLE OF CONTENTS

Introduction 1

Chapter 1: The Abcs From Accidents To Cypres ... 4

Chapter 2: D To F From Da Vinci To Freefall 16

Chapter 3:"G To From Garnerin To Knives 23

Chapter 4:"L To O": From Lenormand Up To Optical Illusion 30

Chapter 5: P To S From Paulas, Kathe To Skysurfing 36

Chapter 6: T To W From Tandem To World Records 40

Chapter 7: "Y And Z" The Youngest Skydiver As Well As The Zen Of Skydiving 48

Chapter 8: Basic Considerations 52

Chapter 9: Reversion Technique 92

Chapter 10: On Piste 127

Chapter 11: Goodbye To The Bad Stuff 163

Conclusion 184

Introduction

Humans have always dreamed of flying since the time they first started walking. If you look back at the history of mankind, you will discover numerous stories and stories of people trying to fly. There's the tale of I carus who was too close to the sun, causing the wax to melt that held his feathers. He sank into the ocean and drowned. Perhaps the tale would be more enjoyable had Icarus had the parachutist...

This book explores skydiving in all its types. From the origins of skydiving, through equipment and record-breaking world events, this book will provide you with an intriguing glimpse into the mostly unexplored world of skydiving.

Two reasons to why this book is amazing

1. The book is laid out in an alphabetical order which makes it simple to locate the subject you're searching for. Each chapter is composed of three or four characters of the alphabet each letter having two or three topics beneath it. After each subject,

there's an opportunity to look up each letter of the alphabet to find additional details related to the subject being studied. For instance after reading about "Accidents" you'll be directed to the subject of "Automatic activation device". After you have read "Broadwick Tiny" you'll be referred to "P" in which you can read about a female pioneer skydiver.

2. Every topic is brimming with entertaining and original stories that bring some entertainment to the otherwise serious subject.

What is the reason for Skydive?

If you're considering skydiving, it's either something you've always wanted to try and it is most likely on your top ten bucket lists or you've been through some difficult experience in your life that made you want to push yourself to the limit or live life to the maximum. Many skydivers do it to find the joy in life once more. As we will discuss in the final section of this book , in the Zen section, Skydiving has the power to accomplish exactly that.

Skydiving isn't going to solve your issues or pay off debts , cure you of an illness or bring your loved ones back. However, it has the ability to change your perception of things. It requires you to let go of your worries for a while and be present in the moment.

How can you make use of this book?

The book can be read alphabetically , or simply go through the book and choose the subjects that are of most importance to you. The subjects covered are selected in order to cover all types of skydivers, including the aspiring skydivers as well as the new skydivers, and even experienced skydivers.

Chapter 1: The Abcs From Accidents To Cypres

Accidents

What is the reason I choose to start this book with an accident? It's because, as an air diver, you have to be aware of the activity you're doing can be life-threatening and dangerous. Every skydive may be the last one you take. This is not a way in order to sound morbid or attempt to discourage you. I say this because it's an actual fact. Skydiving, by essence, involves the process of jumping from an airplane that is in good condition! There are accidents and, in skydiving the chance of accidents happening is higher.

According to parachutistonline.com, in 2012, the two main causes of skydiving fatalities that year were malfunctioning of the main parachute and canopy landings. The website claims that skydiving incidents occur due to a series of events, but it also states that each one by itself is an accident that is waiting to occur. If a skydiver chooses the parachute that is not sophisticated for her level of knowledge or part of her normal equipment the possibility of an accident is likely to occur.

in 1999 Jan Davis, a 60-year-old woman living in Santa Barbara, plunged to her death in protest of park regulations that banned jumps off cliffs , such as the 3200 feet El Capitan in Yosemite National Park. She was fifth of five jumpers participating in the protest , which was organized in protest of the death by drowning of another person who succeeded in parachuting off El Capitan, only to drown in the water below while trying to escape the guards.

Davis her husband, the famous cinematographer and photographer Tom Sanders, was among the audience and he sank onto his camera in sorrow when his wife fell in her grave. The woman was jumping using borrowed equipment because she was not willing to allow her personal equipment to be confiscated by park rangers waiting to take her off the ground in the valley. She typically threw an elastic cord around her back, but in the borrowed jumpsuit the cord was hanging in her leg. An emotional Sanders complained on and off: "If only she had employed her own gear. If she only owned her own equipment."

If a person jumps in conditions of poor weather, accidents can occur. If a person does not recognize the area well and is in the drop zone not a familiar area, then an accident could occur. If a jumper does a low turn, then an accident could happen. Look up "Automatic activation device" below for more information on the method to prevent low pull/no accident involving pull.

There are many accidents that aren't necessarily bad. One particular accident ushered in the modern age of parachuting freefall. For more details, see Broadwick, Tiny.

Accuracy Landing

It's a kind of skydiving which is very competitive in the nature of things.

Skydivers earn points for landing in the most precise way possible an area in the earth. The landing gets most of the focus.

Automatic Device for Activation

This is a small , computer which constantly monitors the altitude and activates the reserve chute when needed. The scenarios in which the AAD could be activated could be: If the skydiver is unable to jump as she gets out of the plane, or while she is falling. If the skydiver loses altitude due to distraction. If a skydiver, or an aircraft is flying too near to the skydiver, it causes damage to her equipment or makes her unstable.

Bailout

The first bailout successful was completed in 1922. Before that, and especially during the First World War, pilots were advised to crash their planes in the territory of the enemy instead of bailing out from aircrafts!

BASE

BASE stands for Buildings, Antenna, Spans (bridges), which is a reference to Buildings, Antennas Spans (bridges) as well as Earth (cliffs). BASE jumpers are skydivers who take off out of fixed structures that belong to any of the mentioned four categories. The majority of BASE jumps take place at a lower altitude, which means that traditional skydiving equipment will not work. BASE jumpers are equipped with modified skydiving equipment to account to the specific circumstances of BASE jumps. The equipment used for parachute jumps and techniques for packing are designed to allow the parachute to fully open quickly. BASE jumps can be created from as low as 200 feet or even 150 feet.

A certain BASE jumper offered this advice: study everything possible about the sport. Find out about weather conditions, the effects of wind and how it does to structures, buildings, and cliffs, and structures so that you know what you'll be able to accomplish and what you will not be able to accomplish.

Bodyflight

It's how you fly your body with control. It involves turns, rolls along with lateral movements, as well as other tricks that are performed in the air in mid-air. Bodyflight allows skydivers to move closer to one another when they freefall to allow them to form a formation skydiving. They then take off so they are able to reach the safest distance needed so that they can release their parachutes.

Broadwick, Tiny

Georgina "Tiny" Broadwick was the first woman to leap off an airplane. She made the jump on the 21st of June, 1913, in a daring act. She was dubbed "Tiny" due to her weight of 85 pounds and stood four feet tall.The following year, 1914 it was the first time a woman could make free fall jumps from an aircraft which was a feat that came about completely by chance.

In the 1913 demonstration jump from a military plane the parachute's line got caught in the aeroplane's tail assembly. It was impossible to get back to the plane as the winds were blowing her around. Tinydid not get scared; she chose to cut only one small piece of line, and then plunge towards the earth. She pulled this line with her hand, and then let the parachute from its closure showing the basic principle that the rip cord works. In the event that she was able to survive this accident she demonstrated that it wasn't required for a parachute to be connected to an aeroplane for it to be opened. This also meant it was feasible for a pilot jump from a damaged airplane and safely land.

She has jumped more than 1000 times from planes. Check out "F" to find out more details on free fall jumps. Check out "P" for additional details regarding women who skydive.

Canopy

Skydivers employ"canopy," or "canopy" to mean the actual parachute , not the entire parachute system. Parachutes of different types are used for different reasons. The more skydivers leap the more, the more she'll have experience landing and flying parachutes, however it doesn't mean she'll have greater control of the canopy. The longer a skydiver is not jumping and then lands, less she has sensation of the canopy and judgment of ground reference. She'll need to make two more jumps to get used to feeling and fly in the same way she did prior to.

It is the weight suspended that affects the loading of the wings, meaning that it is a crucial element to think about when choosing what size canopy to use. If you're not as experienced with skydiving experience, it is recommended to choose a canopy that is less loaded. The selection of canopy will have to do with the skydiver's capability to comprehend the canopy, manage it in a safe manner and respond appropriately when there's an emergency or a challenging landing.

Different types of parachutes exhibit distinct behavior when open. Certain canopies open more slowly than others. The faster the canopy is opened, the greater physical strain will be placed on the body of the skydiver which is covered in the section "Hard closing". Large, high-cambered canopy will end up flying less horizontally, but have greater vertical speed when they touch down, which is landing hard. Colder air has more pressure in the air than air that is warmer. This implies it is that, in cooler climates canopies perform better than those in warmer climates.

Students can make use of canopies which measure as large as three hundred square feet . However, experienced skydivers can utilize canopies measuring less than 100 square feet. Go to "World Records" to learn more about the most compact canopy.

China

You may be surprised to learn that China is where parachuting started around 1100 years ago. It's true that planes hadn't been invented until then However, humans are quite creative. The Chinese would look for natural structures like cliffs from which they could leap from! Many believe that a primitive form of parachute was described in Chinese documents more than 20 centuries long ago!

There is a story of Emperor Shun who fled his murderous father. The emperor sought refuge in a granary. However, his insane father spotted the granary and set it on fire, while the emperor in the granary . According to the legend, the emperor put together a few straw conical hats and then jumped from one of the tower's windows, and lived to tell the story. It is believed to have occurred before the year 90 B.C.

A news story from China was published in which an Arab who stole legs of gold table in a mosque, jumped from the minaret of the mosque. The story says that the Arab survived because he was carrying two umbrellas which acted as parachutes. This particular tale has similarities to Armen Firman! See "F" for more details.

Cypres

A very renowned Automatic Activation Devices is referred to by the name of

CYPRES AAD. Cypres means Cybernetic Parachute release System. The AAD comprises four main components which include the small display along with the computer, the battery, and the cutter, which is the device that deploys parachutes reserve.

This is how it operates. The computer decides that it is the right time that the parachute of the reserve deploy and sends the cutter a signal once this critical time is reached. The cutter's tip is like a knife, it cuts through the closing loop, which is the place where the pin that closes the reserve parachute pierces through to keep the reserve parachute inside the container. When the closing loop has been cut, you can ensure that your reserve chute will deploy. The CYPRES will cut off the reserve loop only when the skydiver is in free fall at 775 feet.

The computer is required to manage normal flying once the main chute is successfully launched; sudden pressure changes have been caused by rolling from back to front or from flying around other skydivers who are free falling or due to weather conditions like the entry of a low-pressure system into the zone.

Chapter 2: D To F From Da Vinci To Freefall

Da Vinci, Leonardo

Just a few hundred years earlier than Lenormand (see "L") Leonardo DaVinci was the famous painter and inventor of the most beautiful art, like The Mona Lisa (around 1503) and The Last Supper (around 1495) made an illustration of the frame of a wooden parachute which featured a pyramid-shaped shape. Alongside the sketch was an explanation that explained what would happen if someone owned an encasement made from linen, where the openings are closed and the size was approximately 23 feet wide and 23 feet deep The person will be able to leap from any height without causing injury.

The most distinctive characteristic of Leonardo's parachute was the fact that the canopy wasn't rounded but was triangular. Many wondered if the triangular parachute could provide enough resistance to air to be able to flotation, and if, with its massive wooden frame it was lightweight enough. Leonardo has never built or tested his parachute , but at the time of his death in 2000 Adrian Nichols did, with unexpected results! See "N" for more details.

Disabled

There's no reason why an individual with a disability cannot enjoy the thrill and excitement of skydiving. But, every disability needs particular considerations and procedures. For those who are hearing impaired, it is possible to participate in tandem skydives however the tandem instructor should be able to converse with the hearing impaired person regarding what is expected of them, like the requirement to put their legs up prior to landing. A interpreter with a sign language background who is knowledgeable about skydiving is required during the briefing. If it is possible the tandem instructor must be proficient in signs and language. Blind people however don't require any special considerations when tandem skydiving.

Quadriplegics and paraplegics are also able to skydive tandem, however special equipment needs be utilized. As of the month September, Lukasz Kufta from Myslowice, Poland skydived from 4000 meters. Lukasz is a victim of SMA which manifests as symptoms of stiff and weak muscles, as well as curvature of the back (scoliosis). The preparation prior to the jump took about four and an hour to ensure that each aspect of his impairment was and understood by the skydiving team and Lukasz was aware of everything was required to be aware of about the equipment to be used to jump.

Elevation

A typical jump height is 13,000 feet, or 4000 meters. This allows the skydiver approximately an hour of freedom. Any altitude higher than 16,000 feet, or 4,900 meters will require the skydiver utilize oxygen supplemental. At 16,000 feet the skydiver will get around 75 seconds of unrestricted fall.

Exits

Imagine you are holding your arm in the window of the car that you're in while driving. The breeze you can feel is caused by the speed of your vehicle rather than the weather. Skydiving is called"the relative wind. Relative wind is by far the most crucial factor to be considered in freefall since it is the only thing to consider when you freefall.

Beginning the second you leave the plane until the time your parachute goes up it is important to think of yourself as a body-pilot rather than a mere man or woman who has fallen from a perfectly safe plane. When a person goes swimming and leaves all their knowledge of dry ground in the dust. Similar to skydiving, when skydiving, you must abandon all that you have learned regarding the earth.

Two important aspects to be aware of when you are considering exits is time and the way you show it. The first is the relationship between the skydiver and others who are skydiving. The latter is about how the skydiver's position is related to the wind's relative.

An arch refers to the body's position that skydivers use to keep an appropriate and neutral posture in the wind. In the analogy of swimming it's similar to the moment you are floating on the water. Skydivers should arc towards the wind in a symmetrical manner; her hips should be pulled forward in the direction of the wind, and her legs and arms should be spread evenly as they are pulled inward. The chin should be raised to create an even curvature from the skydiver's forehead up to her toes. It's similar to lying with your head down in a bowl which is small, with your arms and legs spread in a uniform manner. The skydiver must begin the arch prior to exiting the plane but shouldn't take off since the momentum could cause her to slide over onto her back.

Firman, Armen

The year the year 852 CE, Armen Firman made the silk suit which had rods made of wood. He then climbed up to the top of the minaret of the mosque of Qurtuba and then jumped. The device increased enough to slow his descent , ensuring that it didn't fall at the speed of light. He was a little hurt, but was able to live to tell the tale.

Freefall

When a skydiver dives out of an airplane, she falls into freefall. She can move her body around in all directions. It is possible to fly ahead, but she can reverse and go in a sideways direction. She is able to increase the speed at which she falls, and slow the speed of her fall. She is able to do turns, flips, and even stand on her head, or even on her feet. The fundamentals of freefall are straightforward because just two elements are handled the skydiver's airfoil, or body and wind. Also, Mantis location in the World Records. World Records.

The average skydiver is around 120 miles/hour, but it doesn't feel like being dropped to the skydiver. This is due to the constant force of the aircraft is able to send the skydiver down through a steady arc, which means that there isn't a the sensation of falling that most people are hoping for.

Chapter 3:"G To From Garnerin To Knives

Garnerin, Jacques, Jeanne-Genevieve and Elisa

Jacques Garnerin is the first man to take part to skydiving in the form of a sport. He was the first to do this in mid-1802. It was true that planes weren't invented at the time, so Garnerin took off from balloons. The balloonist was Garnerin, and invented the frameless parachutist. He made use of the silk parachute attached to the basket an air balloon. The balloon was before he skydived up to 1000m above the ground.

He was in a huge basket suspended from a structure that resembled a closed umbrella. In the middle was a tiny hot air balloon that carried him into the air. Once he had reached the appropriate level, Garnerin cut the small hot air balloon. The device that resembled an umbrella with a lid was opened. Garnerin was able to glide back to the ground and was not hurt.

On the 12th of October, 1799, the wife of Garnerin Jeanne-Genevieve was the very first female to go from parachute. Jeanne-Genevieve's daughter, Elisa Garnerin, completed 39 parachute descents in the professional field between 1815-1836.

Hard opening

Hard openings occur the moment when the canopy of the main canopy opens to the outside in a hard way. Hard openings can be very dependent. What one skydiver might consider to be as a hard opening could appear as a normal opening for another skydiver. It is possible to suffer serious physical trauma or death because of an opening that is too harsh. The injuries can range from minor strains, pulled muscles necks and backs that are broken, and even tear-ups of the aorta.

According to research conducted by an organization that studies parachute, an opening that is soft has a maximum force of around 3. A more difficult, but still sensible opening is recorded at 6. A proper packing technique is crucial for an opening that is soft, however there are other elements which can influence the type of opening a skydiver have to face. These include the dimensions and the state of the chute and how the canopy is designed, the kind of suspension line and the speed of freefall, along with the location of the chute for deployment.

Hot balloons in the sky

Skydiving in hot air balloons is a fright to many skydivers. The thing that makes them unique is the absence of wind in the air as you exit the hot balloon. When you make a normal plane jump the speed of air that the aircraft has is high, which means that once the skydiver is released her balloon, she's able to swiftly move through the air. The absence of wind relative in a hot balloon jump means there is no way to control the initial few minutes of freefall. It's like BASE jumping as it is an unweighted drop. It's also quiet for the first 10 minutes or so. Then you can feel and hear the wind speeding up while you gain speed.

Indoor Skydiving

Vertical wind tunnels allow skydivers to enjoy the excitement of skydiving without needing to get out of a perfectly stable plane. Skydiving indoors simulates the freefall part of skydiving. Indoor skydivers learn the art of flying her body over an air column that is produced synthetically within a small space.

Altitude is the most significant distinction between indoor skydiving and traditional skydiving. Skydivers generally exit planes between 13,000 and 10,000 feet up. Indoor skydiving is where this height is reduced. Indoor skydivers enter the wind through a door at the rear of the flight area by leaning forward, and then lying on the wind that has been created.

Canopy is yet another distinction between skydiving indoors as opposed to its more conventional counterpart. Indoor skydiving is where the focus is on the body-flight element of skydiving. Age is the other major difference between the two kinds of skydiving. As young as 3 years old can be permitted to skydive indoors. In the US traditional skydiving is restricted to those aged 18 or over. In other countries the minimum age to participate in traditional skydiving is fifteen years old.

Contrary to traditional skydiving that depends heavily on weather conditions indoor skydiving doesn't depend on the weather. Skydivers in indoor skydiving can participate at anytime of the year. In addition, indoor skydiving does not require the initial "jump" in performed to an instructor. Anyone who is a first-time indoor skydiver may jump on their own.

Skydiving indoors has allowed traditional skydivers develop their skydiving abilities. In the past, skydivers was required to do thousands of jumps over the course of several years to get the experience they needed. Skydivers today can take off for hours at an indoor skydiving center and, since one minute is equal to one skydive, a conventional skydiver can gain a lot about skydiving over a shorter time. This has reduced the cost of learning to skydive in groups.

Jalbert, Domina

Domina Jalbert is known as the creator who is most famously credited with improving the design of the contemporary, multi-celled rectangular parafoil. He first patent the design in 1966 and was the basis for the current design of the ram-air parachute. At the close of the 1970s, RAM air parachutes were swiftly replacing round parachutes. Check out "Ram air parachutes" for more details.

Jumpsuits

The fabric that the fabric of your jumpsuit is made from can affect how it is flown. If your jumpsuit is too large and heavy, it will create more weight on your physique, which means that you'll fly about in the air.

Kenya

Gary Lincoln Hope, the director of instruction of Sky Dive Diani is of his opinion that the coast of Kenya is among the most beautiful scenery around the globe. It is blessed with breathtaking beaches, and the ocean waters that is protected by reefs display incredible colors when viewed from above.

Maybe this is the reason that draws skydivers from around the world to Diani beach each year to participate in Kenya Skydive Boogie. In the 2002 edition of the competition, more than 120 skydivers jumped continuously during a period of two weeks. Because the airstrip was located nearby and a few of the most avid skydivers did up to 19 sky jumps in a day!

The altitude at sea level together to the equatorial temperature results in skydiver's freefall lasts for a longer duration than normal. The typical freefall time is around 30 seconds, however in Kenya's Diani beach the time for freefall is increased to approximately one minute! Sunset jumps are very popular because they offer skydivers stunning views of the sun setting.

Chapter 4:"L To O": From Lenormand Up To Optical Illusion

Lenormand, Louis-Sebastien

Louis-Sebastien Lenormand is credited with being the first inventor of a parachute that was actually used. While inventors such as Leonardo as well as Vrancic (see "V") had created parachutes prior to Lenormand's invention but it was Lenormand who proved the principle of parachute in 1783. He was the first to leap from an overhanging tree and then fall to the ground, without injury because of the two umbrellas Lenormand had altered to fit his weight.

His 1783 leap was constructed with a 14-foot fabric parachute that was framed with wood. He jumped off the Montpellier Observatory and his parachute was able to catch the air, allowing him get to the ground and not be injured.

Love, Todd

Todd Love is a triple amputee veteran who refuses to let his disability stop him from skydiving. In 2013, he'd completed 4 tandem leaps. Todd lost both legs as well as his left hand due to the impact of an IED (Improvised Explosive Device) while he was stationed in Afghanistan.

Mantis Position

The name was given to this position because, when performed correctly the skydiver will look like praying mantis. The neutral mantis posture is distinguished by the arms being over your head in an angle of around 45 degrees. This is also referred to as holding your ball. Your head should be supported, and there must have a little arch in your hips, with your legs extended slightly beyond 90 degrees.

The mantis's position enables skydivers to increase their the range of motion as well as the replication of motion. The term "range of motion" refers to the skydiver's ability to travel in any direction, and to pick up and present grips , without obstructions to their ability to keep control and stability. Replication of motion refers to the ability to replicate the same move successfully repeatedly continuously.

Nichols

In the year 2000 one of the most daring daredevils from Britain, Adrian Nichols, created a prototype that was that was based on Leonardo da Vinci's parachute concept. Then, he tried it out in the month of June of that year in the wide areas of Mpumalanga located in South Africa.. He was dropped from an air balloon which was 3000m above surface. Leonardo's idea actually worked, and Nichols said that the parachute provided an easier ride as compared to modern parachute systems!

He cut himself free once the altitude reached 2000 feet. He the parachute was deployed again that was the current version. He did this to ensure the heavy apparatus designed by Leonardo da Vinci would not fall over the person he was landing on.

Skydiving at night

Before you take a night skydiving, make sure to make a few jumps from that spot in the daytime. You ought to be able to open quite high on at the very least one of these jumps and consider the dangers that could be risks if you fall in any direction away from the drop zone in the night. You'll need a glow stick as well as a flashing light that can be easily turned on beneath the shade. Also, you should be in a dark space without lights for a short time so that you can allow your eyes adjust to darkness.

The glow stick must be connected to the altimeter, or you can use an altimeter with a clearly lit. If you decide to utilize a glow stick you should turn it on prior to beginning making your eyes ready, and then put it on with the duct tape which you'll take off just prior to your leap. This will ensure that your glow stick isn't an error and that the light won't reflect on eyes of people. The strobe light needs to be attached to your body or your device. It is possible to attach it to the side of your leg, the helmet's back or your back, as when it starts to fire your body will be keeping the light from shining into your eyes, even while it's visible to others.

To maintain your night vision, be careful not to look at lights while on the climb to the altitude. It is important to ensure that the jump plane does not have lights in the interior and no one is using flashlights to illuminate the plane. Only red lights should be used inside of the plane since they won't affect you night vision.

One of the most important things to remember concerning night jumps can be the effect of shadows. If the moon is in your back when you're landing, you'll likely be able to see a massive black canopy rising in an exact collision course with you. It is just the shadow you're falling into. Many skydivers have attempted escape turns and then crashed into the ground only to discover later (if they make it through) that they did not avoid their shadow.

Optical Illusion

If a skydiver is recorded on film as she opens her parachute it appears as if she's lifted. It is merely an optical illusion caused due to the fact that the cameraperson is falling as the skydiver being captured slows down because of being able to deploy the parachute. Another optical illusion can be seen skysurfing, a sport. If you observe someone floating across air currents in the exact way to the surfer riding on a wave the reality is that it's an optical illusion created through clever camerawork. If the cameraman keeps her camera in place and the skysurfer appears remain in the frame, even though the skysurfer is falling down at a speed of between 90 to 160 miles an hour.

Chapter 5: P To S From Paulas, Kathe To Skysurfing

Paulus, Kathe

Kathe Paulus is among the most well-known females to have ever been involved in skydiving. In the latter half in the late 19th century she parachuted in Germany becoming famous for her unique display of the skills of an female. Together with her husband Latterman created the parachute model to ensure balloon flight would be safer. The prototype was the initial development of a collapsible, collapsible parachute that it could be folded before being put inside bags. Her husband passed away while she was testing the parachute however she did not die. She made further improvements to the design and earned an impressive fortune during the First World War. In the end of August 1914 she'd completed more than 70 descents using her parachute.

Physics of Skydiving

Two forces are involved when a parachute goes down. The first one is the gravitational force that is what forces every object down to the earth. A second force, the other one is called drag. If an object is connected to a parachute, it is a force that pulls upwards is brought to play with the object. The air resistance to the canopy, which slows the descent of the individual or object.

Ram Air Parachutes

These parachutes extremely controlled gliders. They have left and right steering line and toggles that work similarly to the controls for elevon in aircraft. They're an air brake that is also an elevator when activated in tandem. If you're an average skydiver you can reach the ground within a few yards of the chosen landing area. If you're an experienced skydiver, you could reach within inches, feet or even millimeters from the chosen landing point.

Landings can be as gentle as the skydiver wishes to make them. A majority of skydivers who are sport do not wear shoes for jumping and some wear barefoot when landing zone is grassy or is an ocean.

Sky Surfing

Sky surfing was first introduced around 1986 by two skydivers Dominique Jacquet and Jean-Pascal Oron from France. Troy Hartman, a former sky surfing gold medalist believes that out of all skydiving techniques and disciplines sky surfing has the highest difficulty. Skysurfers must have mastered skydiving prior to beginning sky surfing. A minimum of 200 jumps is required to allow the skysurfer to master how to control the board for sky surfing. Once she has learned how to control her board, she will be able to perform flips or spins.

Sky surfing is one of the most dangerous skydiving methods. If the skydiver is spinning or flipping around and the parachute is opened the parachute could wrap up and become a massive knot. Spins can be so intense that it can knock off the person who is skydiving. Troy Hartman, who is certainly one of the top skydivers on the planet has had spins that increased in speed so that the capillaries inside both of his eyes ruptured and his eyes turned completely red. Skydivers have an habit of tying their arms to keep blood from accumulating in their extremities while spinning.

Chapter 6: T To W From Tandem To World Records

Tandem skydiving

In 2012, around fifty thousand people around the world attempted the first tandem skydive. Tandem skydiving is a great option for those who aren't experienced and want to skydive. The participant is connected to an experienced skydiver , who is qualified Tandem skydive trainer.

Therapy and Skydiving

Skydiving is a potent method of therapy. After the death that his dad committed, an experienced skydiver named Adam Martin decided to go skydiving. His family thought that he was dying, but the truth was the reverse. He was determined to take the risk by skydiving to get himself out of self-destructive spiral. Another skydiver realized that skydiving helped him release his anger and resentment toward the individuals who had abused him as an infant.

Researchers have discovered that people who are experienced "risktakers" like skydivers show less anxiety levels They also have a good perception of reality, and possess emotional control. They also are capable, resourceful, flexible and energized. They are with above average intelligence, with a high sense of independence, assertiveness and assertiveness, as well as possessing a desire to achieve and be acknowledged. Other research has discovered that risk-takers like skydivers tend to be more relaxed and less controlled through the superego.

Studies have also proven that contrary to what is commonly believed extreme sports like skydiving aren't just about adrenaline. A lot of experienced skydivers describe the sensation as a high-level of tranquility. One particular BASE jumper highlighted the fact that BASE jumps brought mental clarity and emotional clarity as well as the feeling of being totally relaxed.

Skydiving can be an excellent confidence boost. The act of jumping out of a airborne plane requires mental focus and mental power. When someone skydives successfully and remembers the experience. Whenever challenges occur it is possible to always come back to how they have jumped from a plane and survived to tell the story.

Vrancic, Faust

The first parachute to be used in practice was invented around 1595, by Faust Vrancic, a Croatian inventor. He called his invention Flying Man (Homo Volans). A few years after, in 1617, the man tested it by jumping from a tower in Venice by jumping off an elevated platform.

Weights

Physics is a major factor when skydiving. That means your weight will determine the speed or slowness at which gravity pulls you toward the ground. If you're thin, you will have to dive close to the edge of your range in a stifling and uncomfortable body position so that you don't lose touch with your skydiving companions.

One solution is to wear weights in order to be able to fly in the most comfortable and flexible position. The kind of weight as well as the amount can differ between skydivers. These two aspects are determined by the body's mass and the actual size of one's body. Other elements that help determine the kind and amount of weight to be utilized include the neutral posture that will be employed and the degree of expertise.

If you're heavier on the lower half that is more so than the upper portion, then an exercise vest could be ideal for you as you're more likely to slip backwards. In the event that your body seems well balanced, then a belt will be ideal for you. It is beneficial when performing the mantis posture. The belt is able to be worn with or without a jumpsuit , but it should not be carried in such a manner which does not block one's hands. Rig weights can be inserted into the rig, if it includes pockets to store weights. It's the size of the rig which will determine the weight you can put inside it.

World Records

In Freefall, skydivers who are experienced collaborate to make different formations , and hold them for a couple of seconds before breaking away in the form and taking their parachutes off. It is believed that the World Record for formation skydiving is set by 400 skydivers. It was kept in a height of 25000 feet, for 4.25 seconds in Thailand. As of August 2014 the smallest canopy that had been skydived from and land at 35 feet, by Ernesto Gainza in Dubai.

In 2013 an all-time record for the most head-down free-fly formation performed by women was established. A total of 63 women joined hands for a total of one and a half minutes to keep the formation. The women were aged between twenty and fifty-two. They clocked speeds of up to 165+mph as they fell upside down, with their heads first, before heading towards the /Arizona desert region. The victims were from Russia and in the U.S., Mexico, France, England and Canada.

American Cheryl Stearns is the person who holds the world record for parachute descends of an female. In August 2003, she'd parachuted 15,560 times. In March 2014, she had jumped nearly 18,000 times. Also, she holds the record for the highest number of jumps in a single day by female skydivers. In 1995, she broke the record and completed 352 jumps within 24 hours.

The year 2012 was the time that Felix Baumgartner became the first skydiver to surpass the sound speed without a vehicle in his leap from 38 miles above the surface. He jumped 843 miles per hour which is Mach 1.25. On the 14th of October 2012 Baumgartner was the record-holder in world history for the most high parachute jump , which was 127,852.4 feet. The following year, on the 24th, 2014, the record was broken with a jump of 135,890 feet, which is over 25 miles higher than the ground. The leap was performed by Alan Eustace, a computer scientist and Senior Vice-President of Google. The two Baumgartner and Eustace required specially-designed, pressure-sensitive, suit of pressure that resembled astronauts because without the space suit, the blood of both would've been boiling within a matter of seconds of exposure to the air-less conditions at such high heights.

Prior to Felix's jump on October 14th the world record held for more than 50 years. The record was set by Major Kittinger who, on August 16, 1960, jumped at an altitude of 102,800 feet. The report said he fell at a speed of 614 miles per hour. He used his parachute to 18,000 feet.

Record-breaking for most senior person to perform a skydive is held by Hildegarde Ferrea, who was 99, made the tandem jump. This happened in the year 1996, in Hawaii.

XTREME

The members from the Xtreme team skydived with wounded veterans into various events. The name stands for "train to rehabilitate, empower inspire, persevere". The organization was transformed to become Operation Enduring Warrior and they continue to help wounded veterans.

Chapter 7: "Y And Z" The Youngest Skydiver As Well As The Zen Of Skydiving

Youngest Skydiver

Skydiving teacher Herman Landsman, and his two-year-old daughter Demie set records in 2001 and Demie made history as the first skydiver to be the youngest in the world. Herman took off from an airplane at 14,000 feet while she was secured to his chest and made the two-year-old Skydiver the most youthful in the world. The skydivers did not have an age limit for Dutch passengers.

Zen of Skydiving

Zen refers to the Japanese method to say"chan," which is the Chinese characters "chan". Chan is actually the Chinese version of the Sanskrit word "dhyana" which can be translated to mean meditation. Zen isn't so much an ideology, but rather an approach to looking at things. It is about becoming aware of oneness with the entire universe and everything within the world (including heaven!). Zen is being present in the moment and experiencing the world to its highest degree. It's about being free of distractions and the imagined conflict of our physical environment. It is about being at one with the universe in all its glory. It's about being present in all its fullness and delighting in the wonder of life.

Parachutistonline.com featured an article that highlighted the peak experiences of skydivers. The article was written by Abraham Maslow, the man who established the hierarchy of requirements, who came up with the term "peak feeling". Maslow defined it as an state which was accompanied by a high-energy mental state which is usually experienced through self-actualizing individuals. The author of the article claims that self-actualizing skydivers take advantage of the skydiving challenges to enhance their abilities. The writer further notes that extreme experiences do have similarities to "flow" the concept created in the field of psychology by Mihaly Csikszentmihalyi.

Flow is among the ideas that connects Zen and skydiving as according to the opening section, Zen is about being immersed in the flow of all the universe. Mihaly defined the flow state as one that is engaged in what he or does that their is able to forget about the world and nothing else appears to be of any importance. This is exactly the kind of experience many skydivers experience. It is an experience that is Zen experience, because as stated in the beginning section, Zen is about being free from distractions and the virtual conflicts that exist in life's physical reality.

Mihaly also notes that when one is in a flow state, it seems like time is flying through the air, a person's attention gets sharper and one is less self-conscious. Successful skydivers are able to prepare themselves to attain the state of flow. The goal is to focus on the goal is to achieve a flawless skydive. Many precision competitors employ the technique of silent mediation.

Chapter 8: Basic Considerations

Equipment - THE SKI

To improve your skiing It is helpful to be aware of the ski, its workings and how to maximize the performance of it. Recent evidence has come into the fore from paintings on walls in China that shows skis were being used as early as in the past ten thousand years. They've developed a lot since when they first appeared.

The ski has become an advanced machine, and you've likely realized that companies who make skis are highly competitive. That means that, year after year, there's always an intriguing technological innovation that is often, a significant improvement in the performance. As of this writing, thinner, lighter skis are hitting the market. There's even one available that features wink tips. I'm not sure what the final outcome will be and I'm not planning to talk in depth the details of a ski's design and design. They could fill an entire book and it's essential to have a good understanding of why and how skis function in the way they do.

Which kind of skiing do you require to enhance your skiing? The past several years saw an incredible improvement in the design of skis. The days of recreational skis are gone that were at least as long as the length of your arm was above your head. The optimal length is anywhere between 5cm (2in) less than what you are, to 5cm higher than you are, as the general rule. It is so well-designed that they can grip the ice, move fairly quickly and even float on powder. They must be lively as well as moderately rigid, maybe 5-10cm taller than your height and have the edges and bases in great quality. The most important thing is to test different pairs and play around with the results.

If you choose to rent or purchase at a retail store ensure that you visit at a time that is quiet. If you visit to a shop that is busy the owner of the skis may look at you from afar and, judging from the expression at your face, which could be pure terror or cool omniscience will hurl a pair of skis without explanation. You can ask the staff at the shop for suggestions. Let them know that you're an experienced skier, and you'd like a pair of performance skis with a hint of welly. The hire departments at ski shops have seen significant improvements in the past few years, which means you'll likely benefit from hiring them if you're just skiing for a week or two. If you're lucky enough to spend an entire season on the slopes, go deep, spend the cash, and get a pair following the advice of a professional or experimenting with an identical pair of skis.

What do you know to buy? If you're looking to try a ski at the shop or from a person you know Take a close glance at them before you buy. Examine the bottoms. Are the plastic soles clean and smooth, free of gouges and holes? The edges must be clean and smooth, with no pit marks. They may have been smashed by previous employers, therefore test them to determine whether there is any life left. Try putting them together from sole to sole and pressing them together with one hand on the mid point , just in front of the binding on the front. You should have a decent gap and some spring as you squeeze and release. The experts will tell you there's much more involved in testing skis at the workshop than this however if there's an absence of spring and no gap then there's not much left in the old ski. To feel more comfortable, you can compare the skis with old battered pairs.

The ski's base must be level without getting bent or warped. Close one eye and gaze down the length of your ski to ensure that it's flat. (Shutting one eye can make you appear more professional rather than having both eyes open.) While the ski is flat when it is in rest, it must have the capacity to turn in motion (called torque) however, that is not appeal to us here.

Be sure to speak to the staff in the shop and inform them that you'll need an all-terrain ski that's going to be a lot of work and they'll let you test out different pairs until you can find the best one for you, provided that you are able to pay for the rental of course! Keep in mind that you'll need to put in the effort to make the most of your skis that are good for performance, and learn the techniques to go with it and improve your performance, so keep reading!

REVERSE CAMBER, ETC.

Let's think about how the ski functions. It's a rather odd form actually. The pointed part in the front is flipped up and the reason is pretty obvious. But what makes this ski (viewed at horizontally, from the other side) is bent upwards toward the middle, and then why is it longer in the front and back than the middle?

There are three terms to think about in this article, and they are "camber", "sidecut" and'reverse camber'. You can take a brand new ski from the rack of the ski shop and place it on the floor flat. The ski doesn't need an safety binding at this point as well, and you don't need to do this in the ski shop if aren't confident, so imagine yourself doing it. Place the ski on the floor. The center is probably 3 quarters of an inch away from the floor. Slowly move it with your finger and let it move fast; it will bounce back up. This is the springiness inside it, just as you would when you pay an eight-week advance to book your ski vacation. The upward bend of the ski is referred to as camber. Take a examine the ski from the top. It's narrower in the middle, compared to the tip and at the tail. This is referred to by the term sidecut. This combination of camber and the sidecut creates the most exciting thing - the possibility for reverse camber. If you know the basics of this are free to ignore it. My view is that it is crucial to improving your skiing.

Imagine standing in the middle of the fall line on a perfectly smooth , steep slope. The lower ski is up floating in the air since you've raised your leg. As you lower the ski horizontally towards it's slope. The first part of the sole that touch on the slope will be its tip as well as tail. However, the center of the ski won't be touching the snow yet due to the camber, which bends upwards. When you drop your legs further and move the center of the ski further downwards it will reach the edge on the entire edge after you've bent it past its straight point into an opposite angle or camber. The length of bend you can make it before the entire edge touches is determined by the extent of the sidecut. The downward arc the ski has now described is known as reverse camber. It's under the tension of an ordinary spring but not much however, it is more than what you could have done it in the shop , because at the shop, you had the ski flat and now it's at its edges. If you begin moving ahead down the slope using only the ski on its edges, the ski will slide over the snow because of the sidecut as well as the reverse camber. Are you able to comprehend this? If not, then read it over and over until you understand it. It's a crucial part of the theory.

We'll discuss this in the future and it is expected to be possible to add reverse camber by adding more pressure at just the appropriate moment, and thereby achieving the type of turn that we only imagine.

Different combinations of sidecut and stiffness determine the kind of ski it's. For instance, a specific one-piece slalom ski made to perform fast turns, has a more sidecut and will be more stiff to give more spring an enormous slalom that is designed for longer turns and general recreation skiing. I've not discussed the effect of length on skis performance, but this is mainly due to the fact that you already know.

If we leave skis for recreational purposes for a second longer, the bigger the ski, the more quickly it'll go. It is also less stable to spin, particularly when it is moving at lower speeds. In high speeds, a larger ski will be safer than a smaller one, and it will become more easy to turn the more speed it speeds. However the largest skis of all at 240cm that are used for speed skiing are nearly impossible to turn even with minimal sidecut and no camber. A sixty mile per hour snowplough is the best method of changing direction on these beasts. Returning to the normal skis and, if using a ski for recreational use that is super fast, provided we maintain it on its edge, but we'll have to do more to come in the future.

In summarising this information, the result is that great pair of skis has the ability to benefit you , as long as you are willing to work hard for them.

RELEASE BINDINGS

They've evolved a lot from the bone-snapping bear traps of the 50s and today we don't even ever think about these. They have also been so advanced that you'll require a rocket scientist to grasp the technical aspects.

I have to admit that I can always identify what skis I had been skiing on however, I would be difficult to pinpoint what the brand name was of my binding doing such a great job of holding me in place and giving me the freedom to move with such ease. There are occasions when, however, they can be a bit off - mostly because they're not adjusted in a proper manner.

There's been a standardised set of din settings for all kinds of bindings for a long time since then, so that the dial numbers of all brands are identical regardless of type of binding. It is possible to adjust them to match the weight and experience of the skier. The greater the number, the more heavy and/or more skilled the skier generally. They must be tightened to the point that within a sensible space they both secure the skier in place and let him free in the event of need. A binding on the back releases in order to stop the skier from breaking his leg, while the front binding lets him know that he is not bending the knee ligaments. There are many reasons to avoid dealing with, a secure back binding was relatively easy to master, whereas an appropriate front-facing binding proved more challenging. This is the reason there are fewer injured legs than knee ligaments that are common today. In general, bindings must be adjusted to match the weight of the skier however, his normal weight and the speed at which he is skiing, and the terrain he's ski-boarding on should also be assessed.

The thing I would suggest is that the person who adjusts the skis on your behalf in the store is mindful of the weight you are carrying and will adjust the bindings to match. If they pre-release and then come off after you've made no mistake, you should check which one is the culprit. In the case of the rear one, it would be open however in the case of the front one , then the back one will remain closed. It is common to borrow a screwdriver from a person at the lift hut, but don't trust anyone else to help you out unless you're very attractive and you do not mind being sued when you suffer a terrible accident due to the wrongly adjusted binding. In half clicks, tighten until you can stop the binding from releasing. The more difficult you ski, the more powerful the setting, but raise the setting by small increments.

There are occasions that the bindings will pre-release in circumstances so unusual that you'll know there's no necessity to change anything regarding the bindings. This occurred to me about five years ago when we were ski-ing in the sun, on good hardpack snow. I took a decision to hold on towards a way that was a bit away from the sun and then hit it a little too quickly. It was classic ice. rough and hard like a ship's bottom , and I realized I was in danger. There was an abrupt left turn around fifty yards further down, but before I got close to it, my right ski slipped off, and it was the ski I required to make a left turn. I was just about to get the ski uphill ready to begin turning, but I was unable to cope with the rough ice and slammed into the lip to the left of the bend around thirty miles per hour. There was nothing visible on the other side of the bend, aside from the valley that was further away. The moment I launched my left ski stopped on the slope and I flew over it. I described an expertly executed parabola that was about 20 feet over the ground in its top point only my boots on and I landed on all fours 20 yards away from the bend, in soft snow. The passengers who came upwards in the gondolas two meters away had a blast.

BOOTS

There are a few points to talk about when it comes to boots, and you've probably heard of them by now. They must be comfortable and secure your heel with a firm grip. If they aren't holding your heel securely, you'll need to move more than the ski and you'll need them to respond immediately to every request. Your toes need to have some movement to ensure that blood circulation continues. There's nothing more depressing than removing your boots at the at the end of the day not feeling any sensations in your feet after lunch and then finding that all your toes changed color to black. It's sensible to own your own pair of shoes as everyone's feet are distinct, and even your left foot is distinct from the one you have on your right. Boots with foam-filled soles are in fashion, so go out and spend some greenbacks. Pick the most expensive boots you can afford. They can last for a long time.

There's still a distinction in the rigidity of the outer shell, but this is not the case for competition models. Do not be afraid to opt for the best boot that you feel comfortable in It will likely appear odd in the store. You should spend a lot of time deciding and then clumping around wearing both boots. Keep in mind that you'll be doing a lot of walking too not just to the lifts and returning from the bar. Once you've completed this book, both the mountain and you will become one. That means you could have eliminated the lift system and be walking on foot, carrying big rucksacks and a beard that is long.

POLES

In reality, you can use any junk poles so long as they're of similar in length, about the same weight and include a basket. I've always regarded fashionable, expensive poles to be a total expense. The way you're likely soon be skiing means you'll be breaking, bending, and probably losing many poles. Many shops will likely add the poles to what you purchase, you'll then be able to spend that extra money on your skis.

However, there is an important point to keep in mind regarding poles. Find poles that are slightly smaller than the length recommended to your own height. This will boost what's called your anticipation and help you get to a lower level at the right moment. Make them two inches smaller, and when the attendant in the store looks at you in a bizarre manner, tell them they're for your little sister which is two inches less than you.

There are other things to take into consideration prior to setting off for Damascus. You might be familiar with a few of them. And if you know the entire list the heavier, practical things will be much less difficult to deal with later.

Fitness

It's not a huge amount work for someone who's been skiing for years to be off on blue slopes for a week, doing poor turns and listening to music through their phones. Don't think that I'm against sloppy turns. It's only that if you're going to improve your skiing it is essential to make precise turns too and that takes the effort!

It is then mandatory to exercise. It is not necessary to be pounding out ninety pounds in the deck of pec, or doing seven-minute miles with a an ounce of lead attached to each ankle however it's recommended to follow an organized and regular program prior to stepping out to the blue, white sky or Scotland and so on.

Do something to boost your aerobic capacity that is, your puff as well as some aerobic work to build your leg stomach, and thigh muscles. Walking on and off hills or walking through them, can help you power and puff. If you're not able to perform this, then a program at the gym with weights, paired with aerobic machines, is the best option.

If you have your own ways of doing things, adhere to them. There's nothing worse than doing an exercises you dislike when you have alternatives to your own. Speed chess and golf However, they aren't of very effective. It's important to keep in mind that for all the effort you do to get fit in the beginning, the first few days at 6000 feet can cause you to feel as if your efforts have been wasted. Don't worry about it. It's worth it. Just think about how you'll feel with those tiny red blood cells rushing through your veins on the first day back at the office.

I'm sure I'm a spoilsport I know, but don't consume too much alcohol when dining on the slopes. It could be beneficial for your calm and relaxed attitude that's why I'm repeating it however, it will quickly destroy any physical fitness and when combined with your reckless attitude towards skiing could transform you into something incredibly risky. Being breathalyzed on a ski slope can be embarrassing. There are of course instances where the weather is getting chilly, there's nothing more enjoyable than being barefoot at a warm mountain restaurant with a good group of people and a blizzard that is in the air and then a ride in the cable car right as the moon rises.

1B 1B BASIC CONSIDERATIONS

STYLE AND BALANCE

I'm often asked by people "Can you help me look more fashionable?' and I must reply "Don't ask me for advice, buddy I'm as elegant as the hunchback at Notre Dame'. I've never really been one for fashion, really. Style can be a jump in the water in my opinion. You can develop an individual style. Everybody develops their own style, ranging from ugly as a pig to gorgeous (the second kind being limited to the more attractive sex) without any thought, however there are those who invest hours trying to improve it, and lots of people think that achieving it will boost their performance. In the nightclub, that is the way to go however not when you are on the slopes. There are times when you'll see a random person descending toward the restaurant. "Isn't Hugo an amazing skier?' asks a person at the table behind him. Here , he is with his legs shackled wearing an shantung pink Versace suit. His arms hang just a little bit from his body as he makes perfect connected turns. His skis are flat on the smooth surface. In the bumps after having a three-course lunch with a glass of wine and three pears Schnapps, and I'd love to know how fashionable the guy is.

Do you think Franz Klammer have style? But not the sort of style that could be taught, he did not. Don't worry about it.

You'll have to compromise style for the high alter for better balance!

There are many methods you can improve balance, but there is no quick fix to mastering it. Balance is based on a mix of miles, what stage you began to ski or snowboard, as well as whether you've played any similar activities that require balance like horse riding or cycling. If you began when you were a young child then balance should been innate and there is no notion of skiing as "easy" or "difficult". If you began late in your life balance will not be automatic until you've completed a lot of skiing. You'll have to rely on strength and endurance to keep you up and keep your balance at first. This will diminish as you gain balance. Another thing that can help to improve your balance is focusing on where your weight is located at each moment and the kind of snow you're skiing on. This will be discussed in depth in the future.

For better balance, keep your skis approximately four inches apart instead of trying to maintain them all together. It doesn't matter how close the instructor is to his skis. He's just trying to look fashionable. It might be difficult to keep the skis on the same level to begin with, as they can be prone to cross however, they'll eventually develop out of this. You can lower them as well. I have always been a firm advocate for using the English Lavatory Position (ELP) for those who would like to utilize it because it lowers the center of gravity, as well as giving the impression of a larger stance much like a low-slung and wide wheeled sports vehicle. It is not my intention to say that it is required for everyone in the process of learning however it seems to work for some. Take note of the fact that you're doing this and it won't last forever If you intend to improve. However downhill racers typically use a more refined version of the technique - somewhere between a controlled turn around gate and a twist.

The longer stance also allows the skier more freedom with their centre of mass that can move to a certain degree over the top and bottom skis. This is discussed in greater depth in the section titled "The Uphill Ski" (ch10).

Make sure to keep your weight on your feet, unless you are told otherwise. Since you've probably not thought about the position the weight of your feet, not even on skis and it's certainly not something people are spending long periods of time thinking about. So, try doing it right now. Simply stand up on your feet, knees a slightly bent and slowly move them in a circular motion, both forward and backwards. It's a bit of a weird way to move your feet in the ball of your foot instep, heel and then back to the instep, heel and back to the ball of your foot not too far however it could make a significant difference to your balance when skiing.

Maintaining your weight on to the mid-point of your feet allows you to have a greater margin to make mistakes before your fore - and aft balance is affected, as well as your longitudinal balance and lowers the upper body by bent knees and hips reduces your centre of gravity, giving you an easier and more stable balance in the lateral area.

It is obvious that when you're playing around in this way the style won't be your primary concern however, as you run under your skis, then the quicker your skis will begin getting closer as well as the better-balanced you be. In short, your style will change, however it is an unconsciously progress.

It is possible to improve your balance by performing a simple exercise anytime during the year. When you are doing your routine pre-skiing exercises why not take a few minutes walking along some narrow area? I built the rail fence of a post in my garden. the top rail is one inch and a half wide and 30 feet long. It was just three feet higher than the ground, and I didn't do much harm when I lost my balance, which happened frequently. I definitely improved how I balanced on posts and rails, however I'm not certain if my balance on the skis was improved! It's something that's in need of some more evidence before I can write it down in stone, but I could tell it did some good for muscle groups in my legs.

I recently had the pleasure of meeting one of my first acquaintances who was practicing t'ai-chi. In the course of an hour's training I realized that this ancient method of Chinese routine exercise was the right thing to help improve balance. It's especially beneficial when we age and the muscles and ligaments that help us stand upright weaken naturally. Tai Chi encourages them to keep working. It also provides us with the ability to see where our body's position is in the world around us as well as being to be stimulating both physically and mentally. The course is taught by a teacher is required, and preferably one-to-one until the techniques are mastered, and then you are able to go by yourself or with a class of other t'ai chi'ers.

FALLING

"What do you mean when you say how to learn to ski? One simply skis or gets tripped up - it's easy as that! Ian Fleming, creator of James Bond, 1928

The high miles you're racking up on your skis will result in at first you'll be falling often. This can be detrimental to your self-esteem as well as your credibility however, at this point as you progress through your new learning process, you'll need to quit the practices.

It is a crucial aspect of the process of learning. It reduces fear and, oddly enough, often helps to prevent injury if done correctly! It is important to learn to be relaxed If you are tense when you fall, you'll harm yourself more. It is normal to fall when you are over your limits. If you're developing a more positive attitude to skiing this is going to happen frequently.

Accept the fact that you're likely to slip and fall often, and you'll learn to take it easy while doing it. I'm 70 and when I don't slip and fall every day at least once ski, I'm not doing enough.

Do not be depressed because you're falling way too often! There will be days when you're constantly falling and you can't ski any more. Accept that. Even the top skiers have to accept it. They generally take the remainder of their day to relax, and go home to read a great book, like this one.

If you've got time to think about it, you can attempt to fall backwards, with your back slid upwards from your skis. Relax while doing it. If you're able that you should keep your foot in place and keep your feet together, this can aid in the process too. This is probably obvious to the majority of people, but it's amazing how many struggle with to get into the most horrible knot. A quick, controlled lay down while both skis are suspended in the air could be the most rewarding fall because it is possible to go straight back up , and everyone looking at you thinks you've done your best trick.

Once you've managed to score several hundred drops (some of which you'll label as bad crashes) I don't have any doubt that you'll be in control of most of the falls as well as a few crashes. It is important to recognize that the other crashes could result in injuries because that's inherent in the sports and I will discuss this further in the future.

BODY POSITIONS

A general rule is that the upper part of a skier's body, including the head, should be facing downwards down the hill. The reason behind this isn't as clear as you've been misled to believe. There is no doubt that your teachers may have forced you to go down the hill in the past and you may have believed that it was just to stop you from going towards the top and preventing you from doing those fascinating things like reverse snow ploughs, skis crossing backwards and on. It is reasonable to think this, but it's only half that's the point.

Here's an example that will demonstrate why your body should look downwards. At this point, treat it as an experiment that is purely hypothetical. You can try it if you aren't convinced by my words, however for the moment think about doing it.

Find a friend who is trustworthy and then hang the tree branch with his arms in order that his skis may be six inches above the ground. Then, grab the skis' tips and rotate them to make sure they're at exactly right angles to your friend's line sight. This should be done until he starts screaming. His head and the majority of his body must be looking forward. If you release his skis (make sure to get them out of the way as quickly as you can) then the skis will revert in their own time back to their original location. In this state of no weight, they can swing back because of the tension that is in your muscles, tendons and muscles of the person you are with. The stomach muscles and the thigh as well as the tendons that hold him together are twisted like a rubber band and for as that as long as the body of the skier is looking down the slope and the ski is turned, it tends to return towards the exact direction even when without weight. Simple , isn't that?

I've mentioned before that generally speaking, the upper body must always look downhill, but there are occasions where it's not necessary and a couple of occasions where it's advantageous to face upwards.

It is essential that the upper part of your body to be in front of your skis' tips while you are cruising on a quick traverse or on a trail that is straight along the fall line, without turning. Perhaps you're searching for goats over you while you move through the snow, but keep in mind that based on the speed you are traveling at, even the slightest movement or twist of the upper part or even your hands or your head, could alter what direction your skis travel.

As I've said that at the beginning of long, fast turns it can be beneficial to tilt your upper body slowly into the slope. This is little more than lifting the arm that is downhill up the chest. However, it can have the amazing effect of turning the tail of the skis around. It's like a miniature stop for christie in preparation to the turn that follows. This process, referred to as contre virage is described later (ch7) however it also demonstrates the torsional power that muscles and the rest of your body may exert on the direction that the skis are heading. You might have seen films of skiers descending down slopes before the start of the war, in which they would make an exaggerated virage down the slope prior to the turn, and turned their bodies to the opposite direction, using an explosive movement of their arm outside. The heavy, long wooden skis of the day easily chased their owners, much like loyal dogs.

Try throwing your body periodically to begin an unweighted turn without steering or unweighting to see what happens. The skis will follow. There will be a few hilarious looks, but when you consider all the other ridiculous things you'll be doing to get better at skiing then who cares?

ANGULATION

Let's look at four dangly parts - the arms and the legs. The key word in this case is angulation. And this is a reference to the same thing, which is that of bending the knees and hips. Its main goal is to position the skis in a position to be on their edges. This is accomplished by bent knees (the lower one is lower than the upper) to the slope, and then lowering the upper body, stretching the hips. This is usually done in a way that the weight is placed in the middle of the feet and the ski on the bottom, however it is not always the case. Variable degrees of angulation could be employed to place the skis in a tack typically in the turns and once you've been practicing this for a couple of days and you'll be thankful that you have read about fitness! Your ligaments and muscles will be getting trained.

ANTICIPATION

If you angulate, your upper body might be facing towards the slope, toward the downhill or someplace in-between, based on the kind of turn you're making. The main factor that determines the position of your upper body, and in a way the amount you angulate is the way you use your poles. Where you place your poles to keep your head in the proper place is referred to as anticipation. I also consider anticipation to refer to the full use of your eyes and the sensitiveness of your feet and I'll explain that soon.

POLE PLANT

If I refer to pole plants, the general rule is that it is constructed vertically, unless specifically stated. This means it is able to be positioned in the snow anyplace on the downhill side within an area of approximately 2 feet away from you lower boots. The further away it is from the snow and the further away you have to angle.

According to me, this pole is likely to be the most crucial thing that a skilled skier should focus on when learning a new techniques. Everything else follows But more on that later. Thus, going through the process yet again:

It is important to anticipate turning in order to lower the pole in the snow horizontally. A majority all of the load will fall on the lower part of your foot. An angle can get your skis closer to the edge, and in this, it will allow you to have more precise control when turning. Then you will be in the position to get ready for the next turn in the event that it is necessary. The speed at which you accomplish everything is dependent on the kind of turn you're taking.

How you utilize your eyes and your feet are also aspect of anticipation. It is essential to be aware of the terrain you're skiing on and what you're going to ski, to be able to react in a manner that is appropriate. It is therefore essential to be looking ahead to determine the speed you're traveling, so that you make the correct choice. The feeling of the snow you're skiing on is felt from the soles of your feet. It is a feeling that tends to increase with time and knowledge. It's an interesting activity to close your eyes for a few seconds each now and then (preferably in a wide-open smooth, quiet and uncrowded piste) to get a feel for your feet. This topic is covered in greater detail in the section about snowcraft.

CARVING AND EDGING

In the article on reverse camber, I explained that the ski is constructed to act as springs. Based on the design the ski is able to be bent to create an extensive arc that is reverse camber. For instance in the case of a racer performing sharp turns on ice using Slalom gates, they will need the skis bent to the maximum extent to make an arc around the gate, with the least amount of sliding. For the gates that are easy to access towards the end when the turns are nothing more than wiggles, the racer will put the skis along their edges with a minimum reverse camber. Edging is the process of putting the skis on its edges while carving applies the pressure required to cause the ski to bend further than the minimum reverse camber. In order to achieve the highest reverse camber, one must not only apply their weight to the center or back of the ski. It is also applied more often to the front by moving a little towards the front at the beginning of the turn. This can cause to the side of the ski initially and the process of bending gets amplified, and then transmitted back to the ski.

It is a great moment to discuss another thing I discussed when I wrote about reverse camber. In the event that a skiing ski gets placed on its side, it will contain more spring as opposed to if the ski is in a flat position on the sole. There is also the possibility of having further reverse camber and, consequently, more spring. If you ski flat on the snow doesn't have the chance of a reverse camber, which means there is there's no spring to guide you through the next turn.

A ski with edges will perform a more precise turn than a ski with a flat surface could ever. Imagine that you're skating. What control will you have in your turn improve an ice-like ski or one that has the edge cut into? The answer is clear. A few years ago (well more like thirty years ago) we used to prepare skis to run slalom gates with a scraper. We would do this by scraping their soles of the skis with a scraper made of metal that was sharp, and then bending it slightly as we removed a portion of the sole made of plastic. This resulted in it was the case that the sole would end with a slight concave. The thought was that the transition between edge and edge will take less time and take less time on the flat surface of the ski, which would allow for greater control. When running flat, the ski would be more stable. stabilization in its direction. It was not clear if it worked in practice. I'm not sure. The only thing I can remember was scraping a number of ski soles right down to wood!

Self-Assessment

In the UK it's an euphemism, which brings up the question of HMRC Her Majesty's Revenue and Customs, but in this book, it signifies exactly what it states in the book, and if you'll permit me to stray for a moment.

Self assessment can be utilized to help test your performance in any kind of sport. It is a good idea to ask yourself "How proficient am I in skiing What are the types of categories you are able to select. They are clearly defined enough to prevent cheating and getting yourself a higher grade or, as is the situation that you give yourself a lower grade out of modesty!

Unconscious Incompetence

Conscious Incompetence

Unconscious Competence

Conscious Competence

The Zone

The term "conscious" refers to your brain. The "competence" is to relate to your body. The "zone" has connected to nirvana and complete enlightenment.

Take a moment to think about them. The very first stage of unconscious incompetence is the one of a complete novice. Do you remember what that was like? You didn't know of what you were doing as well as what you decided to was most likely to have been an accident. You were instructed to do something by your instructor or a colleague and your brain was melting down. If someone was to ask you what the duration was during the time your trying to carry out an action, most likely, you didn't notice the question. In essence, you didn't have even a clue about of what you were doing and what you were doing wrong. You didn't care, did you? It was so fun ... wasn't it?

This next phase of Conscious incompetence, is the place I believe the majority of people are. When they are on a good day, they might occasionally progress to the next level for brief periods, but they are not able to make use of this rapid improvement. In the majority of cases, they are acutely aware of their mistakes, however they are unable to improve their method. They are aware of the problem, but they aren't able to fix it. It's often a difficult stage and it's for those who suffer from it that this book is geared.

Stage three is similar to lifting off your first time in an aircraft. I'm not sure what it is, but feels good from the spot I'm in. Unconscious Competence is an amazing first-time experience for those who are a keen skier. And as with many other experiences, you'll remember your first experience for the rest of your life. Being thrown by the skis between turns in a short span of time is thrilling. The thing is that you don't know or know how to do it places you in this category of transition.

Conscious Competence is a fun roller coaster that can take you forward two steps, and back one. It is possible to begin looking at skiing from a different angle and feel the essence of it. It's a lot of work, but you begin to put more effort into planning skiing, learning how your ski operates and why it's more enjoyable to ski on different snow surfaces, as well as computing and integrating into your sub conscious your methods that you use to ski on the different surfaces. This book will assist you in gaining consciousness!

It can't give you the steps to getting to the Zone. It's something that cannot be taught, but it comes from all you've learned, and it isn't something you get often. It's the time when everything is perfect The bright sun shining through the clear sky and onto the stunning snow, the scent of wood and pine smoke in the clear air, and then you're able to ski the most perfect course every turn is the most unforgettable dream!

That's enough now, let's try a method of reversion.

Chapter 9: Reversion Technique

Do you recall what it was like when you first put your skis on? Do you remember the first few days of bruising as well as the excitement of speed that you could not control? I've tried to remember the way our instructor got us moving, but with no luck. I do remember his name and the amount he drank during lunch, and that his face was very bright red smile in afternoons. But nothing else. If you started long time ago , you likely don't have a lot of memories as well, so get ready for the reversion treatment! If you only started an hour ago, everything will instantly be familiar.

This section focuses on the process that brought you moving up into the paralel turn. This is meant to be a revision to allow you to return to practicing it and then think about how it functions. It should be easy since you will no restriction on your thinking like fear or a poorly fitting boot (like you had when you first started).

This will also give you an idea of how you can guide beginners. This is not intended suitable for beginners to read before skiing on the slopes for the first time because nothing else can be able to do the process of learning well unless you get out onto the slopes to experience the excitement, terror and sheer joy of skis sliding across new snow on the first attempt. I have previously mentioned the most basic rules to teach when teaching, so if you can find a any reason for you to teach someone else, do consult these guidelines.

You must practice these fundamental techniques on your own as they don't require an extended time to go through. Perhaps you could go through a few while waiting for your buddies on lower levels of your Gondola. They'll provide you with an understanding of the position of your weight over the skis, the movements you are doing to control them, and the way you're unloading them prior to turning - all useful information to keep to use later.

THE START

Put your skis in. The flat surface is perfect in order to experience the skiing. Straight down the most gentle slope, resulting in an easy stop of perhaps 20m. Side-stepping, with tiny steps to climb to the top of the mountain (going slightly greater each time). Straight down, running straight back up again, using step turns for a change of direction. This exercise should be performed without poles.

The SNOWPLOUGH (Stem or Wedge)

In the snowplough, you must get into the position using the poles. Alternately, the instructor in reverse may be able to hold onto the edges of skis to begin with. This allows the skier to glide down the slope while alternately snowploughs that break as well as straight running. Poles can be held however, the arms must be placed on the skier's side, neat and relaxed. Knees ought to be bent slightly.

THE SNOWPLOUGH TURN

The basic turn can be completed using poles or not at the beginning. By leaning on one ski and then moving it into the snowplough the ski that is weighted will turn. The weight then transfers onto the ski that will turn an opposite direction. It is important to note that the weight stays on the ski that is outside till the turn that follows, meaning that the skier is able to feel of weighting downhill ski.

Different instructors use different terms to describe the snowplough's steering actions however the instructions and demonstration should be as easy as is possible! I show it with an exaggerated lean of my upper body towards the outside ski. Sometimes, I'll be dropping my hand my thigh, pointing at it, and then declare 'Steer the Ski Round'. Some may use the phrase "Drive the ski around" or 'Push on your outer ski'. These will generally work, however there are two things to be aware of.

The second is that the skier will move his weight back the uphill ski after the downhill ski has made its turn. The skier then lies down or his newly weighted uphill ski slide across the middle of his downhill ski and is thrown down on his face.

We've all been there and it might occur to you later on in the event that, for instance, you're skiing over bumps. It's usually a matter of sceptical fear instead of anxiety at this stage because the brain is unable believing that the right slope is for the body's upper part to lean forward and down the slope. The problem usually gets resolved after a short period of time and usually is only seen when turning the other way. It is because one brain hemisphere dominating over another, or something similar to that.

The second issue isn't as severe, but it could result in more severe problems in the future. The body is temporarily frozen in catatonic mode with arms flailing and poles pointed rigidly towards the sky or in another direction. The skier needs to be encouraged to keep the hands of his side. Rest of the body must then follow in the same direction and be relaxed.

Since he skis more quickly, there will be less weight on the ski that is steering. It is essential to choose the slope wisely. It must be wide and smooth with as little people as is possible.

If you're unable to just wait until you've been through my earlier advice regarding how to instruct an untrained person and you want to test these turns on a person now, be sure to keep this in mind:

Instructions should be brief and it must be noted that demonstrations will typically have more impact on the development of a novice than speaking words.

It is crucial to not increase the confusion of the brain of a beginner because that is taking place naturally when he is trying to comprehend the situation!

THE STEM TURN

The process of early learning was developed to bring an order from chaos. The different stages of turning techniques have been categorized into specific actions - the Snowplough and the Stem Turn, the

Stem Christie along with the Parallel Christie.

Many instructors recognize at the beginning of their career they are in a state of chaos, confusion often take over the minds of beginners A strict system of instruction does not always produce the desired outcomes. Some students need none of the instruction. In one instance, I was taking two 30-year-old beginners on a ski trip in the Austrian Alps. I was having trouble with the clips that were on one of the pupils' boots when the other one chose to go off on his own. He stumbled down the slope in a semi-crouch skipping a little with his arms in the manner of a decent imitation of the Snowplough. At the point he completed using the chairlift (about five minutes) the skier had fallen through barriers like the Stem Turn barriers and had been performing an acceptable Stem Christie and is able to maintain for the past fifteen years.

The the fact that he was my brother may have was a factor in the impatience of his brother However, it had taken me three days as a novice at the ski school reach the level which he was able to reach within less than an hour and with not even a single word of instruction!

I seem to be straying off but the main point is that our brave snowploughing novice doesn't necessarily have to worry about the precise steps even if his method, however simple, appears to be progressing naturally. He might already be performing an unintentional Stem Turn.

It is a simple process. Stem Turn involves little more than sliding the uphill , unweighted ski into being in line with the downhill ski with weights after a single turn. The ski that is uphill is slid into position when the lower ski has passed the fall line (the most steep part on the slope) It allows skiers to experience the thrill of traversing without needing to do it from a snowplough position. The weight has to remain on the ski that is lower throughout the entire time and is a good thing since there is an urge to let the skier lean backwards and down the slope. There is also the possibility of lifting the inner ski to join the outside ski; this is not a bad thing since it makes him apply his weight to the ski that is lower and may transform into an incline in the future.

THE STEM CHRISTIE

It is a Stem Christie combines a stem and a christie. If you believe it? The Christie part involves weight reduction and keeping the skis in parallel for the major portion of turn. Stems are used to initiate turning, then after getting to the line of fall, the unweighted ski can be slid line with another in order to give the christie a finish. The beginning of the turn, a pole plant typically used to plant an anticipation seed, increase angulation and also a small unweighting move.

In a traverse, the ski's outer edge is put to an upright position. While doing this, the skier bends slightly in the hips and knees, and then sets the other pole in the opposite direction from the inside of his ski. When the stemmed ski that is weighted closes in on the fall line, the skier is lifted up. Inside skis are brought parallel as the skier climbs up. The turn turns into a christie because the originally stemmed ski has been weakened due to the up motion. The skier continues to turn along the line of fall as well as from his upright position, the skier falls down to plant the next pole.

It's the theory but in actual practice it can be quite challenging to connect the pole plant on one body part and one plant with another. If the student is unable to master it the pole plant could be avoided until they master it. Christie as well as the Christie stop.

However, there is one major issue with Stem Christie as an athlete can be the victim of its great success. It's an easy procedure that is easy to learn in its most basic version without the need for any pole plant, that is only a simple stem to initiate the ski on the turn, and then a slide into the inside ski shortly after. Once it is mastered, it will become the core of the skier's repertoire. As you increase your mileage the upper ski is able to slip into the ski quickly after a tiny stem has begun to turn down the other ski. The result is an inverse (christie) move. If the pole plant is taught at first, it's soon abandoned because there is no technical justification to place the pole since the ski that is weighted is controlled by an angled stem. After the pole plant is eliminated, there's no angulation which means less effort, and skiers can contently spend the rest of their lives ski-boarding down well-groomed pistes in the sun without a concern aside from being late to your lunch time rendezvous.

It is believed that the Stem Christie should be the final chapter in the story, and the goal in this novel is to bring many of those skiers that have used it for a long time to the new world that is available.

THE CHRISTIE OR PARALLEL TURN

This is the stage that beginners are most likely to learn. Though it is not utilized a large amount by those who found it to be the Bog Standard Stem Christie and adhered to it, it's an ideal for a solid foundation for more advanced techniques. The primary difference between this and the previous turn is that it does not have a stem. The skis are in parallel all the time, and they are not weighed by a slow-down and up fast motion.

There are three pre-exercises to do. The first is a parallel traverse using the skis switching between flat running, with the skier standing straight, and a small angulations into the slope to place the skis along their edges. This is a bit difficult for the beginner but it provides him with the feeling of snow sliding beneath the skis when he moves both forwards and sideways using the flat running and also a sense of edging when he makes angulations. If the edging becomes too difficult, it could be overlooked in this phase.

The other exercise is the christie stop which is a slow straight descent along on the drop line. The skier angles right over skis when the skier descends to insert the pole in, then is then able to come up to the pole. Pole plant is vital lies between the top of the boot and the top of the ski inducing him to shift his weight up at the beginning in the turning. When he turns along the fall line , the skis break by sliding side-to-side onto the snow. A lot of weight is placed on the ski that is lower. It is also recommended to practice this on the other skis.

The final exercise is to alternating pole plants when stationary. It is vital as it forces the skier to descend and then come back up to free the skis. Teachers may also have their pupils leap the skis' backs off the ground when they rise. It's quite exciting and should not take long to get over.

The parallel turn can be tested in motion, moving down to place the pole, up and around it, then back down to plant the second pole to get ready to go on the following turn. A couple of turns must be connected to form the basic rhythm. The main issue is not weighing the ski's lower part enough towards the end of the turn because most skiers tend to lean toward the pole plant, and then end up staying there. This is a problem that should be avoided!

There is also an inclination for the upper part of the body to be positioned in a square position against the skis. I do not think this is worth fixing until a skier starts to rotate his upper body toward the slope. However, there are experts, especially in Austria who insist on an unambiguous upper body towards the slope, even when the slope is interspersed with lengthy traverses. It's important to urge the skier to keep his ski uphill only a few centimetres to the left that of their downhill skiing during the traverse, as this will hinder an upper part of the body turning to the side.

This is also the beginning of your learning process. It is likely that it has brought back the way it was in the beginning and gave you an ideas of what you're doing today.

Through analyzing the fundamental movements learned by beginners then you'll be prepared for the next step.

3 - SOME THEORY AND EXERCISES

I've spent two weeks with the regimental ski team that was practicing to compete in the British Army Downhill Championship, in Champery, Switzerland. There's nothing particularly interesting to say about this, you could consider however, there were two men taking part had skied for six days! The event took place one week later and the two skiers finished the course at speeds 60-70 mph, and they didn't even make it to the top. How did they manage it? They did it because they were very fit and were able to accumulate a massive amount of miles and were extremely positive. But without having been taught anything more than a snowplough at beginning of the six-week period they were able to ski downhill.

Some critics might suggest that their ability towards the end of six weeks may have an element to do with affluence that is the British taxpayer. Some of us could argue that it was due to being fortunate enough not to be trapped in the system of ski schools.

The reason for this is to demonstrate that technical expertise isn't all that matters. With complete commitment to the three primary elements of fitness, miles and attitude, proficiency will come easily in the course of a brief period. The issue is that it might be difficult to follow the commitment of soldiers because of time, money or any other reason. In addition, their schedule of training did not focus on downhill skiing as they did eventually become ski instructors however, they took a bit longer to master the art of the various types of turns, apart from those that were downhill.

Modern turn techniques were created in the latter half of the 60s by the leading gurus at the day by analyzing and dissecting the smallest movements of young children and racers when they raced down slalom course. George Joubert and Jean Vuarnet from France captured images of racers using motorized still cameras. Their actions were broken down into create the foundation of the turning techniques we employ today. These radical changes to technique were made in tandem with advances in manufacturing skis and ski boots and, over the last thirty years , the technique has stabilized and been accepted almost everywhere as the best method to ski.

In passing, I hope that the things I write on these pages can spark some discussion, and not only from the theoreticians or teachers who are out there. I'd like to hear your thoughts. It's one thing standing with someone on a mountainside and show them a technique they could execute however I don't have any idea if writing words will produce similar results. Let me know!

Now we're off. Let's summarize the functions of turn:

"The turns are the movements through which a skier changes his course. A good skier utilizes the turns as sparingly as is feasible'. Vivian Caulfield - 'Skiing Turns 1922.

They are used to go around corners. We utilize them to brake and regulate our speed when we are on the piste on bumps, on steep slopes and powder snow. These are typically quick, snappy turns. There are also quick snappy turns to substitute for traditional courting rituals, or when we feel energized with a lot of energy. However, we perform fast, long turns on broad empty slopes, and also for off-piste and glacier skiing in Spring snow, or whenever we are exhausted and can't be bothered to make quick snappy turns.

Our method will be determined by the weather conditions, the kind of snow and even the mood of a specific day. It's all very evident, however it is shocking how many skiers use the sole turn that they have in their arsenal, which is the common stem christie, in order to try to deal with the different scenarios. There is nothing against the standard stem christie. It is a great turn and is the foundation for all the other turns that follow however its popularity as the universal turn may be the skier's downfall. For instance when he attempts to utilize the turn on frozen surfaces, on the steep slope, or in the heavy snow conditions, or even to race around the slalom gates in an event day or a club day, he's not likely to be able to use it in a positive way.

Simply put, you're likely to be able to forget the standard stem christie, and begin the process over. The knowledge and experience that you've gained can be helpful but don't think about drawing on it. It's time to return to drawing.

How do you turn a SKI?

There are numerous ways to turn a ski and the majority of them rely on either steering or unweighting or, as is the case most of the time the latter, or a combination of both. (There is an alternative that is third in which you lie on your back and turn both of your skis around while in the air and also your bottom as well, and then you realize that you're facing the opposite direction as you rise up.)

UNWEIGHTING 1 'THE DOWN SLOW and UP QUICK' METHODO

Then you go down slowly and then leap the back of the skis. Once they're unloaded they can be flipped to the other side. The jumping becomes relatively easy after you get knack of it, and the faster you get the more time you'll have to lift the skis. At the time you read this, you'll probably have mastered this step and likely to be doing only a minimal unweighting. The method is utilized to learn parallel turns, making short, linked turn in snow that is deep and also by giant slalom skiers who have small variations.

UNWEIGHTING - 2 "THE DOWN Quick & UP Quick" METHOD

If you are able to drop down your skis near the end of your turn, they'll unbalance and fall off the ground. If you aren't convinced then stand on the weigh machine (preferably with no skis or boots except if you've got a big bathroom) and fall down rapidly. The dial will go to zero, before coming back up and registers higher than your usual weight. If you quickly drop it as you complete the turn, the skis lose weight and they will slide around slightly further (rather similar to a miniature stop for christie). The weight of the skis is then re-increased when you get up and then brake against the snow. The skis will follow and then you leap to the top and then round. This is a much superior method to the first method for certain turns, however it's more to work. It is employed by racers in slalom and Flash Harrys on the slope, as well as on steep, hard slopes that are off the piste. It is also a method to use it after having mastered "The Basic Short Turn' technique. Don't worry if you aren't sure about this technique right now but it will become evident later.

UNWEIGHTING 3 THE MOGUL BUMPS Method

The bumps take the weight off the skis. Since the middle of skis are positioned over the top of a bump both the back as well as the forward of your skis are lifted out of the snow or, at the very least they will only be slightly touching the snow. The skis are able to be rotated on their center points, provided you are doing other things in addition to those discussed in the Better Bumps Technique. This technique surprises, surprises, is only applicable to bumps, and is an excellent method in learning how to ski on the bumps with confidence.

There are three ways to change the direction of the skis through unweighting, which is lifting either or both away from snow. In the first two ways, there is the reverse of the skis that is typically unweighted. In the bumps technique it's either the front or both the front and back, with the weight remaining over the middle.

STEERING

All turns require steering and some of them began by unweighting the ski while others require steering alone. The process of steering involves adding weight the ski in order to get the ski turning.

Based on the type of turning, skis could be driven along its edge (edging as well as carving) or at the sole (sliding). You've probably figured out the fact that steering your ski along its edge requires angulation and some effort while driving a ski using its sole is a way to ensure that it is easier to sit up and enjoy a more relaxed. The result is usually lots of sliding, and little or no edging novices, as well as a lot of edging, but very little sliding when you are with Henrik Kristoffersen[1[1]. Most novices rely on steering to complete the full turn, while advanced skiers take off the weights of the skis to begin the turn and then guide them through the turn to complete it.

Watch the skiers who are coming along the freeway that is homebound in the evening. Take note of the way they're turning. In the event that the angle is demanding, they'll be using various combinations of unweighting and steering. Check to see the person who's doing which. Don't be fooled by the fat lady wearing a lilac jumpsuit who's skis off and is going down.

4. - PROACTICAL WORK

LEADING Positions

What you're about to discover now is how you can maximize the performance of your skis by getting them close to the edges. The exercises and turns that are in this section will form the foundation for every controlled turn.

To improve my skills, I often suggest a few odd postures - like that of the ELP (English/Global the lavatory posture) and an extended stance are clear examples. There are other variations like the extreme pole plants and the angles over the skis. They should not be used indefinitely, and over time and mileage they'll hopefully disappear , to be replaced by an organically acquired style that one can only imagine right now.

Their importance at the beginning but, it is essential and makes learning much simpler.

EDGING Exercises

There are a few important points to be made before we begin. If you've downloaded "The Secrets of Skiing Better' on the internet, it is difficult to follow these tips to the slope. In this regard, I've tried to make these as easy as is possible. A couple of times will give you an concept of what you need to do. You can print the pages in one go and carry them along in an inner pocket or you can put your laptop and place them on over your head.

In this book, I've spent much of my time talking about certain points. This is deliberate as certain instructions are so crucial that with just one or two repetitions, you could be unable to remember the details.

If you've gone through and comprehended the section on carving and edging in Basic Considerations, you will remember that a ski needs to be positioned on its edge in order to be able to turn in a controlled way. Also, the ski requires pressure applied to its middle in order to create an effective reverse camber position however this will happen naturally when you have plenty of miles and isn't an issue.

Let's begin the actual things. These exercises will introduce you to edging and getting an understanding of the control edging can provide before you begin making precise turns.

Make sure you are on a broad blue open run that has beautiful white snow which allows you to speed enough without worry.

Are you there? Or have you noticed that the lift has broken down yet again? Keep your back straight and standing against the line of fall. Check your skis. Have the bottoms of your skis been flat? If so they are, then you must look for a slope that is a bit steeper to ensure that the edges cut into the ground while you're standing almost standing up.

While sitting there while standing there, lower yourself on the ski's bottom, like you are trying to fix an ankle buckle.

When you walk down the stairs, you must aim to get the middle of the outside of your lower boot. Have you reached it yet? Lower it! Let the pain go! Take note of what has happened to the ski's lower part. It's even more on its edge. In order to reach this position, you required bending your knees towards the slope and to a certain extent , your uphill knee too. Additionally, you have to stretch your hips. This is known as angulation and is an exaggeration for what you should be doing by the conclusion of each turn in the near future.

(Some instructors refer to this posture when skis are in motion , as driving the skis around'.)

If you have practiced this workout in a halt in the opposite traverse and also on the other traverse and now you are able to take the chance to try the next practice, which you might have tried before without having a idea of why you did it.

Begin moving slowly along the slope of your preferred route.

While you're traversing across the slope, slowly lower to the point of your lower foot as you would in your standing position. This will help to edge the skis and place the majority of the weight on the lower ski. Moving while doing this exercise is a bit more challenging than you think when done standing still. However, doing it in a seated position is straightforward. The brain is somewhat more difficult to take an unmoving ski in its teetering position at first, however, if you persevere, it will eventually come.

Stand up and keep all the pressure on your ski that is lower You should see that the skis are sliding sideways and forwards on their soles, which is they are they are flat in the snow.

Begin again, bringing your knees to your foot on the bottom. You should have your knees dipping into the slope, so your weight remains central across your foot. Stop, turn and repeat the process on the next traverse. When you're touching your boot , there will be no sliding in any way, and if you are lucky enough to get the snow right it is possible to glance back and observe how smooth it is, and the slightly curving trench which the edges have created.

A LONG CONTROLLED Turn

This eliminates the practice. The next step is to make a correct turn. Start your left traverse like you're planning to make the right turn first. Begin with your right hand halfway down until it is touching your boot. With your body still in this position, extend your right arm roughly horizontally, and then place the pole into the snow. It's really nothing more than a brief strike in the snow about to the ahead of your ski as your arm outstretched will allow, and approximately twelve" far from the downhill slope. Once you have put the pole in , it will begin to raise it. Then, rise fast enough to remove the weight from the rear of the skis by making a one turn parallel to allow you to begin turning them around. There is no requirement to allow the backs of the skis to be lifted from the ground. In fact, you should use as little weighting as feasible in your upward motion to keep the control. The faster you speed up, the more easy the process will become to lift the skis' backs.

In passing, I'd like to be aware that when you make a directional arc to insert your pole into the ground or in the previous exercise , you make an angulation to get your boot in touch and your upper body will be inclined to face downwards down the hill.

Your speed will increase when you reach your fall line. Try to turn as smoothly as you can, then drop down slowly so that you grasp the left boot with the left hand. This time, use the left. While doing this, apply pressure the ski's lower side.

"Applying pressure" refer to the feeling like you are pushing very hard on the ski by putting your thighs and leg muscles to in the mid-point of your toe. It should feel like you're driving the skis around and that the entire movement should be smooth and steadily.

Why would you want to apply pressure in this manner? With time, and speed and less weighting, this downward pressure will push the skis into a reverse camber. This is likely to allow them to cut through the turn. Furthermore, since they're bending under tension they'll provide you with the chance to bounce to the next turn when you begin unweighting again.

(You will see that I've used the expression "applying pressure" in reverse commas. This explanation isn't going to be accepted in the realm of the realm of physics, but you'll know what I mean once you get started. It must be an unweighting of the lower ski, as you make your way back following the slow upward unweighting motion, and when paired with the turning motion of the ski's edge, a satisfying reverse camber can be made.)

The skis shouldn't be pushed around when you approach the fall line. And from above their tracks , they should appear like the shape of a well-rounded capital S once you've completed a turn on your second route. When you turn after the first turn, and begin to turn, the inside edge of the ski below will begin to bite. Continue straight ahead and then return after you have put the left ski in to speed up towards your fall line then proceed down again smoothly and steadily. Continue for a few minutes before stopping. If you aren't getting the grasp of it then stop, consider the issue, then try again.

It is likely to start to that you might be sliding more over the skis' soles instead of carving the edges. However, as you get used to angulating more and apply more force to the lower ski, it'll begin to be a biting force. There is a distinct section of the turn where the skis reach the fall line, and then pass it while they're lying flat on the snow, transferring across the edge from one side to another. This is the section of the turn where it is the most difficult to keep an evenly round S to Simon. Make an effort to allow the skis turn smoothly when they're sliding across the snow. In addition, it's virtually impossible to make a complete turn without sliding, but if you find yourself in need of a challenge, maybe you'll be the first to accomplish it.

There are two aspects to be aware of when taking this time. First, you must avoid the most common error. When the majority of people are on the fall line, and begin to accelerate the turn, they will accelerate the turn in order to break their skis that are flat as fast as they can in the direction of the drop line and then slow down. This can make things more difficult rather than more efficient, so it's essential to be able to accept and accommodate this speed increase.

If you're looking to build an increase in confidence, in that regard, locate a steep section of track that will lead to a flat or upward slope. Try doing a straight run through the steep slope following an end-of-turn with the knowledge that you'll find it possible to stop quickly and get rid of the maximum speed you're capable of achieving during any turn on the slope. Do you not love the sensation of speeding up with the wind blowing through your hair and your eyes watering so much it's hard to see what direction you're heading?

The other thing to do is ensure the upper part of your body from your hips upwards to the hips, is looking down the hill as far as feasible. Instead of making an effort to walk downwards at this point (after all, you've got many other things to think about) Make the effort to be aware of the area ahead of you, where you might be heading for the next turn. The faster you move, the further ahead you ought to be scanning. Should your head be pointing downwards, then it's safe to suppose the upper part of your body might be facing the same way. It's okay to be in line with the skis, but at this point your upper body shouldn't look towards the hill.

Chapter 10: On Piste

"The British off-piste skier's an avid fan. Skiing for him is an exercise in hard work and the pleasures of hot chocolate, the steaming hot bath and rigid gin are more intense because they're very well-earned. Of course , he loves ski in soft powder snow, but he balances rougher with smoother more philosophically than the majority people, and is not in the habit of letting poor conditions affect his plans. "Often, you can get the most enjoyable skiing when you're in an open whiteout', says the man will yell as he pours porridge before dawn.'

Adam Ruck - UK Sunday Telegraph 2002

POWDER SKIING Technique

It's all about It's the White Stuff! It's no longer a race down the track trying to stay clear of all the other people, and especially the big lady in the lilac shellsuit since this is freedom man This is the best. This was the way the idea was explained when I first was urged to venture out into the snow that was fresh and powdery. It was thrilling, demanding and totally different from what I was used to.

Before you take off to the snow it is important to answer the following question: Are your ready to start over once more? Yes? You should read this article. It is possible to master the art of it in a matter of hours. It could take some time however, in the event that you study this next section slowly and carefully and follow the advice and follow the instructions, you'll be able to ski powder. Before you attempt it, I highly recommend to read this section about Avalanches. This is not meant to turn the skier off but to provide you with an understanding on what's considered safe skiing and what's not.

To be successful in deep snow, you need to be able to ski smoothly and be aware of the way you're doing. You need to be in your balance since the snow is constantly trying to catch the outside edges of your skis whenever you attempt to move them. It's like you're trapped in tram lines but if you succeed in turning the skis, the edges of the skis will sink until they stop and make you fall out of the window.

I'm going to play sexist here. The girls seem to have grasp of deep snow faster than guys. I believe the reason for this is because they are more gentle with it and this is among the reasons why they can ski powder. Take it easy as you treat it with the gentleness that you would treat the spider that you are taking out of the bathtub.

The time is now for business. The exercises listed below are very important and should not be ignored.

1.) Find a fresh, unspoiled snow that is steep enough for you to run down at a moderate pace. (Don't think too much about those who pass your with beards and shouting at you to not ruin their angelic pee.) By putting your weight to the side and on both skis, slowly bounce back and forth. The skis should sit about four" apart. It should feel like you're bouncing upwards and downwards on a trampoline as the snow is compacted on your downward movement. The trampolining effects are the reason why powder skiing is magical. The snow has to be knee-deep at a minimum in order to get the bounce effect.

Let me repeat exactly the position your weight should fall as you learn the techniques for deep snow. Your weight needs to be slightly in the back of the middle of your foot, which is in the direction of the heel. I don't think it's an ideal idea to push the skier to rest on the skis' heels as you attempt to go for the deep slopes. The skis will be more likely to accelerate and you won't be prepared for the next turn in a timely manner and therefore, you should not lean back! When you are getting the hang of skis on powder your weight should shift forward towards the middle of your feet.

2.) Repeat the exercise and this time, alternate right and left poles as you descend. Check your balance is in the right place. The distance your body travels upwards and downwards is vital. When you descend to insert your pole your head, make sure that your head is nearly level with your hand! This is a long way down. Be aware of the driving analogy when doing this. Keep your hands straight ahead of you and look down the hill.

3.) The next step is to turn, so choose the slope that's more steep. It is recommended to choose a more steep gradient than the groomed slope with the same slope since the deep snow can slow the speed. Sit at the top and attempt to remember the pattern of the exercise you've just completed. Repetition it while standing. Down, left pole in, up. Down left pole in, right pole in the up. Left pole, right pole, left pole, right pole. Be aware that your body has to remain downhill at all times and your weight must be equally distributed on both skis, and slightly to the side towards your heels, and the skis are not able to remain flat in the snow. So, you're off. Let's suppose you're starting with the right direction. The weight of both skis. Continue down to insert the right pole into. Make sure to come up and, when you are up you can jump your skis over the line of fall. (Keep the skis on the ground.) In the same pace, begin to drop down right away for the next turn. place the pole in and jump up and round using the skis. Keep your body in the direction of the hill, keep your skis level and keep the pace running (count on your own) and keep going riiiiight every time. (I haven't yet said it, but you'll be able to unweight the skis using the 'down slow, up quick' approach while you're learning. Then, you will be able to progress with linked turns into the 'down fast and up fast mode')

After seven or so turns, you might be exhausted trying to keep a an ideal balance, working your hips, knees shoulders, and stomach and juggling all this with an incredible concentration. Relax to breathe the refreshing mountain air, take in the silence and reflect on how lucky you're not in the bank's manager's office.

It is likely that you are tired quickly as your muscles are doing their best to counter the challenge of maintaining your equilibrium. It is essential to focus on 'Balance' as well as to be able to think "Rhythm", and to think "Gently". If you're making more headplants than turn and you are not getting enough turns, take an extra break until you've recovered. It's an excellent idea to test some deep snow near the slope at first to help you return to the slope and increase your self-esteem for a bit. Do not stay on the slope for too long, and then get back to your angel poop before anyone else snatches the entire thing.

Let's summarize the key aspects to learn how to ski in the powder:

Be sure to balance your weight evenly on both skis

(a couple of inches from each other).

Then, go right to the bottom of the pole.

Maintain your upper body pointing downwards all the time.

Maintain a steady rhythm, i.e shorter connected turns (like windows wipers).

Be gentle.

SKI THE STEEP JUMP Turns

After you've learned this powder technique, there is nothing that will hurt your ego more than a little So let's get to some serious macho. Have you stared at the couloir and thought"I wish I could be that good I could do that!'? In the opposite way what number of times gazed at that couloir and thought, 'Gosh. It scares me. Let's have lunch'. If you've reached this stage in the book without the need to undergo the midst of intensive treatment then you're well-prepared to take on the challenging slope.

Be sure that you have the right conditions. Most of the slopes with the highest slopes are off-piste and may only be skied safely after the snow has been melted and frozen several times, forming a smooth surface. The best time to do this is the beginning of Spring. Select a sunny day, and be sure to check the weather forecast and the avalanche risk and also your insurance.

The best time to tackle the steep slope late during the winter is in the morning after the snow's top layer is softened by sunlight, but not enough to render it unusable and vulnerable to avalanches. First, choose an open slope, not couloir. It allows you to consider going out of the way if you need to. It must be away from the distractions of the miserable piste bashers. It is best to choose a slope that is smooth without any rocks or trees that are a result of miscellaneous obstacles like chamois or marmots.

The slope must exceed 45 degrees for it to be considered steep, and 55-70 degrees is considered to be considered extreme. Try not to go beyond 55 degrees as a starting point. It should have a slope that is concave and have an outrun that is gentle.

This means that should you fall, there's nothing to be hit during the descent and you'll eventually come to a comfortable end with only an ego bruise.

One of the most important rules in the mountains is to never go by yourself off the piste, which means you must bring a companion. I say "must" since a friend could be a burden. You may have hiked up the mountain with the idea of enjoying a quiet picnic under the pines with your favorite friend. The incline you've stumbled upon is just a bagatelle.

To get into the mood, take a few deep breaths and take in the scene. 'Oh look. Is that not the Matterhorn in the distance? Let's go following this. Oh, take a look. It's it. It's the North Face of the Eiger. Let's take a look after lunch'.

So, you've taken several deep breaths, re-energised you, then spread a generous layer of factor 90 on all exposed areas you are now cautiously moving sideways and slipping back to your preferred starting point. Stop. Look. Think about the route you'll take that is closest to the line that falls as you can. You will be going as slow as you can in your connected braking turns. The plan is to begin every turn by using perpendicular poles around 18" (yes 18 inches") away from the side of your lower ski boot. This will help you can carry your weight down the slope. As a rule of thumb the more steep your slope is, the more downward you need to put your pole in. That means that your weight should always be over your skis. Imagine that you placed the pole close to your boots, your skis are more likely of moving away from you when you rolled them around. Your weight would be pushed uphill, as well as behind the skis.

Now, you're standing with your skis in exactly right angles to the drop line. They've created their own small ledges. In order to maintain total control at the conclusion of each round, skis be in this position in a split second prior to the beginning on the following turn. Did you remember learning about the short linked turns back in the past? If you were on a slope that was gentle, the edge sets would have created an outline on the snow similar to this:

If they are on a slope that is steep, they'll need to create the following pattern:

If the slope is very steep, the skis are at exactly right angles with the slope's fall line. This is a good position to limit all forward slides of skis, and can break the skis. Actually, you'll be sliding side-to-side to the edge set in such a way side slip and edge set together should look more like:

Now back to the essentials. It is now time to angulate over your lower boot and plant the pole similar to how you do it in bumps, but you are probably 18" away from your boot. To move the skis around you're doing an easy down and speedy up without weighting. When they reach the fall line , your weight will begin to move down over the ski that is lower and then you'll angulate down to form an additional pole. While this is going to require some effort, it should be completed as smooth as you can.

Make sure that your skis are close to the ground and reduce the amount of jumping. This will allow for a more comfortable stopping as you descend to that next pole. Try linking at least five or six turns before stopping to take an interval. Be sure that your skis are braking 90 degrees to the fall line in order to limit the forward movement. This will make sure you're going down the mountain within an extremely narrow space that is not larger that the skis' length. You'll notice the fact that your body's upper part is in the direction of the mountain when you make the jump turns. This can aid in allowing the skis to move when they are not weighted. (Remember the torsional properties of your tendons and muscles?)

If you are confident enough, you are able to try the narrow couloir which runs underneath the cable car. In that particular couloir, it is not necessary for with you a companion as someone inside the cable car will be able to summon the ski patrol or helicopter.

There are some important aspects to be aware of

Select a slope that is free of the rocks that would otherwise need had to go away.

The best thing to get your hands about is the spring snow that hasn't been exposed to sun too long on it.

If you're off the beaten path, ensure you're not on your own.

OFF PISTE IN SPRING

As the season moves towards the beginning of spring, snow conditions undergo a fascinating transformation. The snow that was cold, clear due to the fact that the daytime temperature was at or below zero, is now transformed into what people refer to as sugar or slush. In the daytime, the sun increases the temperature of the ground when its rays strike the mountain, and crystals of snow melt down into little more than small blobs. The process begins at lower elevations however as the day progresses along, it shifts towards higher elevations and then eventually to the glaciers. What is of interest to the more experienced skier is the high-quality of this material if it is you catch it at the right time.

The spring snow may not be as thrilling like powder snow, however it's extremely pleasing. The nighttime temperatures remain below zero in the morning, and the snow has melted completely. If you give it an hour or two of sunshine and warm temperatures, the top layer, maybe about an inch, is melted and turns an incline into a naturally formed, prepared piste. There aren't any bumps, no icy patches or other created obstacles. It's a beautiful skiing surface.

The glaciers are high up and the transition takes place too. Fresh snow that fell earlier in the season and crevasse crevasse openings that were hidden, now melts and freezes numerous times in order to create solid bridges that cross what could otherwise be deadly man-made traps. This means that glaciers are able to be skied early at the beginning of the day with relative security.

If you choose to have a vacation that is late and you find the majority of the snow at the base of your resort is gone bring a picnic to take a trip to the glaciers or any other place in the clear blue sky. I generally utilize the lift system in order to reach the highest elevation possible and generally begin by taking the first lift of the morning.

Learn about the safety of the region prior to your visit and, if needed you should carry a large-scale map. Do not or your group ever attempt to go on a glacier ski trip by yourself without an instructor unless you've done a thorough assessment of the condition of the terrain or the terrain of the terrain using a professional with local experience. If you're in any doubt, hire a professional who is knowledgeable of the terrain. This will take a bit of money but when weighed against the potential for an expensive rescue mission should you fall through an embankment, or worse the possibility of dying, a guide wins hands down.

Many ski shops will give you two skins as well as some rundonee bounds. Skins roll up and are glued to the ski's bottom. They're made by humans and are similar to bristles that allow the skis to advance so that you can climb mountains and not slide back. They attach to ones that are already attached to your skis and allow your skis' heel to ascend. When you're at the top and are ready to take them off, they are put back in your bag. Do not attempt to ski down using the skins. They could ruin a great descent!

There's not a huge amount of method to consider. It is important to keep an watchful eye on the layout of the road, since it's not difficult to fall into an unintentional cul-de-sac even using the largest scale mountain maps. Check that it is sunny and clear with a clear forecast. If the weather does get closer, you'll be left on your on your own. Pay attention to the ahead, and be sure there's nothing on the slope which could pose a threat. There will be some terrain that is steep, while some are easy. Since the snow is so tolerant, you'll be amazed by the best terrain you've ever skied. That's not even counting the challenges of off-piste!

In addition, sugar snow is the fastest to ski on. It is believed that every piece of snow that exists in its half-melted state is covered with water that surrounds it, making it much more slippery and slippery than the snow that is at less than freezing. This is great news for speed skiers who have broken many speed records for this type of snow.

It could take some time to determine if the weather is going to be appropriate, so be sure to look for what I've got to say on snow kinds.

SKI THE STEEP POWDER

It is only possible to ski powder of 50 degrees or more. If you go higher than that, the snow is likely to slide off even in more stable weather conditions which then becomes an issue of getting down to whatever base is. If you do throw caution at the winds, you may end up coming down during the avalanche. In general, limit the deep and steep slopes that have plenty of trees scattered around. This can reduce the risk for an avalanche. Trees also have the benefit of creating a further obstacle in navigating them.

The steepest slopes of powder are ideal when it is to waist-deep and is more thrilling and can slow your speed in a good thing. The braking power of snow hitting your legs, skis and thighs, as well as your waist, means you don't have to turn around the line of fall when you make jump turns and the braking motion down the skis could be more comfortable.

You'll need to spread your weight evenly across the two skis. it might take a bit of time to find an agreement between weighting just the lower ski and the weight of both skis equally. It is important to find an acceptable compromise between the simple snow skiing techniques, as well as the slightly more difficult technique required to tackle a steep, firm slope.

The way you bounce and the distance into the snow that you drop as you're bouncing, will help to stop your. This will determine the amount of snow that falls across your face and on your shoulders. Wear goggles. You'll require them. If you're not an elite swimmer and have your breathing to match your movements, make sure you keep your mouth shut aside from a scream in pure joy over the sheer fun of the whole thing.

Many people fall off their skis in the depth of powder. If the chance of an avalanche being moderate, it's recommended to wear some sort of cord to your ankle and affixed to the ski. In other instances, I've managed to hold my skis on by diving head-first down the slope just as I was in danger of falling! It takes a little time to clean the snow from the open orifices however it is much better than getting stuck in the poop of angels up to your neck while trying to find an un-modded ski that's likely got slid into the valley that is next.

It is equally important to be aware of any weather condition to wear a reflector or transmitter that can assist rescuers in digging out your body, in the event of an avalanche. In that dark and bleak state what should we do next?

7 - ADVANCED 7 - ADVANCED

A LONG TURN VERY FAST Introduction

I learned to ski in the Norwegian resort, where mountain ranges were more of steep hills and the longest ski runs ran for half a mile in length, cutting narrow swathes across the Birch trees. Curved turns of a short length were the norm for the day (and occasionally, the night). After arriving within the European Alps I was amazed to see vast open trails running down the mountainsides for miles. Short turns were off at the moment; long turns that were fast were on the agenda.

However, speed is just as risky on the road as a loaded firearm when it is in the hands of a five-year-old without knowing how to utilize it. Have you encountered? What is the number of times you smashed into someone other than yourself? Have observed people who were completely in control speeding across the mountain?

SPEED SAFETY

What is the speed you think you are skiing currently not counting the time it takes to start that tuck in the middle of blue runs? 10, 20, 30 mph? It is likely that you are not doing faster than 30 mph but have you considered what you'd be doing in the event of hitting a tree in this direction? Even at 30 mph , you must be aware of people, rocks, snow machines, however, how can you be able to anticipate such issues in 50,60, or even 70 speeds? The large lady in the lilac suit could be a hundred meters ahead, dabbling and dithering, but what can you do to avoid her at 60 speed? It could be hilarious in the bar following the event when you remember the moment you jumped straight over the skis' front up in the air for god's sake, shouting "Banzai!".

Another possibility, that does occur, is that you end inside a wooden container.

It's now common practice in certain Stateside resorts to breathalyze those who are dangerously skiing This suggests that it is a direct analogy to driving in a car: Be conscious of your speed Maintain your distance - Look out for your fellow skiers. Know your reaction speed - Know your stopping distance and reduce speed when you are in dense traffic. As responsible skiers, we need to put these comparisons aside to make them automatic and don't require thinking over again. It is then safe to practice the skill.

For all the turns that are fast, pick a wide, blue, empty run on a Monday, when the weekenders are gone. Be sure to observe the entire course that you will be working on prior to stopping. It doesn't have to be higher than 25 degrees at the beginning. There aren't any weekenders hidden behind those hills and snow machines pushing around blind corners? Good. If it's cold, put goggles on. Nothing is more painful than being blinded by tears while driving at pace.

THE LAZY Fast Turn

Begin your fast traverse. Your upper body may be facing towards the tips of your skis in contrast to the quick turns. Since you're ski touring on a relatively smooth slope there won't be a necessity of edging, therefore you'll be standing in a straight line with your hips and knees slightly bent in front of the skis to provide some shock absorption and keep the upper part of your body a comfortable position to begin the turn. The skis will be nearly smooth on snow.

To start the turn, you should now prepare to rise into a straight position while moving your weight inwards towards an imaginary point that is 12" towards the downhill side on your tips. The projecting action will accomplish two things. It will firstly remove the weight from the skis' back, and secondly, since the body of yours is towards the downhill slope the natural tension of your body is brought into the equation. When the skis turn towards the line of fall Apply a slight force forward to the inside of the ski that is downhill. This will assist you turn more easily. The faster you move, the more efficient your turn.

If you start the turn using a stem, you're in a way cheating.

Find an exact arc of the snow. There shouldn't be any pushing down to the rear of the lower skis in order to bring the skis in a circle against the fall line , and thus break the skis. This lazy turn was created to help you feel of accelerating towards the line of fall. It's of any practical application. I typically use it towards the end of the day , when I'm trying to return home fast and don't have enough energy to angle and tuck the skis into better-defined turns.

This turn shouldn't be taken on a busy piste.

Keep in mind that your weight should be slightly in the direction towards the middle of your foot.

The Fast Turn - - EDGING

The same turn that you did before, however at a higher altitude so that you are able to benefit from those skis' edges, giving you more control. Select a smooth red slope with no too many bumps. It is essential to provide enough angles to keep the skis in the right direction always, except when you climb to turn around across the line of fall. As you make your way around, apply pressure on the front of the downhill ski while you angle again. This is the fundamental slalom turn that racers use and when you have sharp edges, it works just as well as it does on good stuff. Similar to the lazy speed turn that you can do with your skis on the ground, this one is not made with brakes in mind, since it is carving the majority of the time. As the skis move towards the line of fall, there is the possibility that they could slip sideways and lose the exact control you're trying to attain. To prevent this, here's an exciting thing the an lateral projection.

GIANT STALLOM TURN and LATERAL PROJECTION

Since you first started skis, you've been told to put your weight in the lower part of the slope. For this is the first time (officially) you will be able to go uphill on your ski. Do these two exercises to get an idea of how it's like

1.) Choose a gentle gradient and slowly move across it using flat skis using the weight of one ski. Transfer the weight onto the upper ski, but leave the lower ski resting on the floor. Do not overdo it unless would like to rest. Explore for a while. Make sure not to stop the skis from moving forward , with no sliding sideways.

2.) Do it with a slope that is steeper where you are able to use the edges and angulate. It is likely that you will be cutting along the outer edge of the ski's upper edge. The slope will be climbed upwards with steps of approximately 6" every time.

If you're bored by this, go on the skis at a rapid pace, gulping over the ski that is lower, make a leap into the uphill ski and while doing so move your upper body the same way you did previously moving forward and up towards the fall line, while keeping your body weight on the uphill ski. When the skis get closer to the line of the fall, it is transformed into the downhill ski and shifts from one edge to the next. When the ski is changed from one side to the next, you start to press the front with an angulation.

The step-up accelerates the turn by cutting down any braking slip on the ski that is lower before the start in the turning (see the term 'contre virage'). It is extensively used by racers of giant slaloms to increase height when racing, and also by slalom skiers to achieve the same reason. It is also a great way to increase your height while you're navigating through a mountain range, and you realize that you need to climb in addition to moving forwards to get to the restaurant where lunch is served.

It is evident that stopping after completing some of these fast turn is an art itself. It is more secure to reduce the speed to a couple of short turns, and apply the brakes gradually, prior to getting to a stop. Straight into a typical stop for christies at 40 mph, your head and shoulders nearly to the surface, as well as snow sprinkling across the sky, is a recipe for disaster.

THE POWER TURN

It is the most exciting turn you could make, and is only experienced on super GS or downhill. If you've been fast enough during the previous turn , then you could have an idea of the turn. You'll need a laid out wide blue to red piste without any obstructions and most importantly, there are no trees either side. You must have a clear view of about two hundred meters.

The primary distinction between this and the previous one is that you're probably moving ten to fifteen miles per hour more quickly, which is between fifty and sixty miles per hour. To be able to reach this speed during a traverse, you'll require to remain in the tuck the majority all the time. Your weight should be evenly distributed between the two skis , but as you turn, you'll need to shift your weight onto the ski that is uphill. While in the tuck position and speed, this can cause pain to the muscles of the thighs. It is best to only raise your body enough to get started on the upward ski turning before lowering into the tuck again when you reach the line of fall. Your body will be putting its weight upwards and downwards towards the inside of the turn . when you turn you'll feel the energy getting stronger. It makes sense you're running on their edges throughout this turn (apart of the edges shift) however, there is not much reverse camber that creates the long radius that allows for a quick turn. If you are able to do it right, it's as if you're being thrown around in a bucket at the other end of rope. That's how I imagine it's like to never been thrown around in the bucket.

If you are able to practice, it's possible to make the edge change , without raising to lift the skis. When you project your upper body back and then down the hill and back, you should be able to make them turn. If you don't get up, you'll keep your aerodynamic position during the tuck, and will not slow down.

If you begin to get into trouble, come from the tuck, and utilize the air brake on the upper part of your body. You'll be able to control your speed more when you wear an unflattering anorak.

A word of caution! Turns should be performed in a controlled manner and not haphazardly on a ski slope with skiers who are skiing slower ahead of you.

CONTRE VIRAGE TAIL SLIDE

Contre Virage (literally in the French "against the turn") is a great choice to play at the bar at day's conclusion, and is an easy move. It's all it takes is to bring your hand that is downhill up toward your chest and then bringing it back down in a small circular motion. If you're going quickly enough, the back of your skis will begin to slide around. This can be an effective braking effect because the skis turn against the fall line and in conjunction with angulation, can result in an extremely dramatic effect. You could also utilize it to start an edge set before making short turns at the conclusion of those long , fast turns we've just described.

What is the process? This time it's your normal torsion that is at work. When you raise your arm upwards and your shoulder turns slightly, then the muscles on the side of your body, the thigh area, you lower leg and your heel and then you'll see you see the tails of your ski. You might recall that you can create the same type of tail slide using the swift fall from your body during the shorter turns. The results are the same but there are different techniques with different turn angles. Contre Virage relies on steering, whereas the rapid drop is dependent on the weighting. (back to lateral projection)

SHORT Turn WHILE Using LATERAL PROJECTION

This maneuver is limited to ski slalom gates. However, it is likely that you will train through gates whenever you can, right?

Lateral projection on the slalom course can be used to increase height as well as speed up. It occurs immediately following the edge has been set by the bottom ski and is nothing more than an attempt to transfer weight onto the upward ski prior to it reversing into an angle that is the drop line. It doesn't appear that much gain in height, but when the slope is steep, the transfer from the lower ski to the upper ski could result in significant effects when a racer is at a low gate (when when combined with the avalement) and, theoretically speaking, can be more efficient. We have observed this on the long, fast turns when the weight remains on the upper ski, which is then the ski with the weight on its outside during the turn The edge change occurs from one edge of the ski to the opposite. This creates an easier transition going from that edge to the other.

To conclude this chapter, it is possible to combine this lateral projection with avalement, which permits the ski on the uphill side to accelerate into the turn . This is the jet turn technique that I refer to below. The turn becomes an elongated (step) jet-turn, utilizing the lateral projection as well as the ability to avalement. It's interesting, even if it's a bit complicated isn't it?

The WEDEL TWINS

These turns don't receive my vote as practical, and shouldn't be confused with shorter swing turns that we've discussed before. They are linked turns performed on the flats of the skis with minimal edging as well as no weighting. They defy the usual rules of unweighting and steering and instead rely on a waggle at the bottom, with minimal knee angulation both back and across the line of fall, and a gentle upward push on the heel of the downhill at the conclusion to complete the turning. The upper body remains right over the skis and faces to the front, and the skis pivot in to the center of your feet. Wedelling can be employed to create beautiful tracks with just the smallest amount of freshly fallen snow. It is quite attractive when you are with your buddies at the bottom of the ski, but it's not likely to help you get from trouble when you're on the ice or on the steep or deep powder. I once skied with a guy who was able to wedel at such a speed that his back and legs were in complete disarray. He was walking a little similar to. Do you recall the Twist in the 60's? Wedelling has a lot in common with it was on skiing.

JET TURNS

Jet turns are often utilized by slalom racers in order to avoid difficulties, and also to accelerate. It is frequently used by those who are experimenting with bumps.

As you approach the edge setting on the swing for a brief turn and then try sitting down and putting your weight of your heels. The best way to sit at is with your legs and thighs at around 90 degrees. This is what the bumps did for you. Now, you have to make it yourself by putting yourself on the back of your skis. After you've done it once, you'll likely fall down unless you can get back up.

In a slalom course that is steep If a racer is too low at the gate, the racer may attempt an arc turn, and then toss his body down the slope at the same time. The skis have a fair amount of catching up since they are trying to describe an arc that is wider around the gate than the upper body. This is why he increases the speed of his skis in order to catch up. Jet turns are enjoyable with some air at the top of a hill but most often not, they happen unintentionally when the skis speed up down the other side.

Chapter 11: Goodbye To The Bad Stuff

It is only possible to overcome your weaknesses as well as other internal influences only if you are aware of them and are ready to take step. It may sound simple, but do you have any idea what (besides your technical skills) holds you back from your improvement? The fear of being afraid is the first thing that comes to mind, and perhaps even poorly fitting ski boots. However, should I mention 'ski school' or "holiday" are you amazed?

A lot instances of negative influence can become positive when you identify them and address them and you'll find there are interactions among many of them.

Fear, fitness, and falling

"I've been very scared at times, but I've employed this fear to be a motivational factor, rather than let it engulf me Sir Edmund Hillary - 'View from the Summit 1999

I haven't crafted this sub-title solely to demonstrate its alliterative qualities however, I have done it to show that the three components are interconnected in addition to demonstrating that their positive elements are the three primary factors that affect your skiing. If you are able to sort them out and then act upon the three factors, you've almost cracked it. Do you really need to be a genius to achieve enlightenment and nirvana?

It is the single most frequent obstacle to better skiing. After 30 decades of skiing instruction,, I haven't found a simple solution and I don't think there's one.

Don't confuse fear with anxious excitement. The adrenaline rush of nervous excitement creates the desire to move. When you're on the move then you relax and businesslike, and everything seems ticketyboo. The most terrifying form of fear is an emotional and physical weakness that is, inability to move and the muscles being in a tense condition of inactivity, as you fret at the mogul fields that is ahead or the cat as well as the bill from the dairy and so on. If you slide into the sand when you're in this condition, things you wish wouldn't occur almost always will.

Loss of NERVE

Begin by dividing anxiety into two distinct states. First, determine if it's due to a insecurity or nerve loss. They are somewhat ambiguous words to describe similar feelings. It is possible to take action regarding a loss of confidence, however losing your nerve could be irreparable.

Most those who have been successful at one particular sport will end up losing their vigor. They realize that they are unable to cope with the physical and mental demands, and usually take the appropriate decision to put down their skis or to put down the fishing rod. The ones who persist often put themselves to suffering, and a ski vacation should not be as miserable!

There are those who want to go skiing with ailment that is pathological, such as vertigo and agoraphobia. (I actually have had clients who suffer from these phobias to instruct!) They have not been able to provide appropriate guidance. These issues should be addressed by someone who is more knowledgeable than me.

There are many who have lost their vigor due to various reasons. The birth of children can decrease women's thresholds for fear to the point that, even though they're able to go on easy skiing, they've no attraction to anything physically demanding (and I do not have to mention the raising of children).

Some might have had a traumatic fall or even an accident or even a car accident, and the physical harm and pain, even following recuperation, could affect their psychological well-being too. The loss of nerves due to accident and injury is a possibility to reverse in a certain degree but so long as an athlete is willing to accept the limitations of his mental health and accept his limitations, he will still be able to be a pleasure to ski down the gentle slopes. In the majority of cases, after a serious accident, skiers will come back to be even more successful in the future, which is particularly true with racers. This has to be related to pain thresholds, fitness, and other aspects which I will discuss later.

If you come to the decision that skiing in the alps isn't for you, I'll tell you that you've made the right choice! It's a tough difficult sport that is tough and if you're looking to excel at the sport, trying to figure it out is not going to get you anywhere.

Maybe I should add an introductory note about cross country skiing because many have found it to be a more acceptable way to ski for their particular needs. It offers many of the advantages of downhill skiing but without the problems. Nearly every resort in the alpine offers trails through the woods, and around the lakes. You can even greet individuals, and stop and discuss nothing with strangers at any time you'd like. It's a easy, friendly type of exercise and relaxing, and is very easy to master. The majority of ski schools have instructors that have the right qualifications and often, after a busy year of teaching, I've gone out on cross country skis to end the season and welcome spring.

For those cross-country skiers that read this and are dissatisfied with my comments about it being an exercise that is not strenuous, I'll reiterate that it isn't a hard sport. In terms of competitiveness, I would compare it as rowing for an 8. It's a nightmare while doing it, but amazing when you're done.

FAILURE TO CONFIRM

If there's nothing we can do to prevent loss of nerves, there's plenty to be done about the anxiety. In some cases, lack of confidence can lead to the loss of nerves however this is something to avoid at every opportunity! Do you find yourself physically feeling on certain days that you are unable to take a specific slope, however on other days , you are able?

However, you do set in the hopes that something might happen. The skis are skipping all the time, you're relaxing and the forecast is awfully grim. There's a chance you've got some hangover from the party the night before after you've finished all of the Resolve. Then you get hit by bump or ice, and wow! The smallest amount of confidence or "go" that you were experiencing earlier disappears. It's a physical state not an emotional one. It is often caused by fatigue or any other physiological issue. Whatever the cause the physical condition affects your mental state to the point that you feel a sense of being inadequate. You have two options; it is possible to either get dressed your bags and head home and take the smart option, or you could continue to blunder until you start to panic and even lose your nerve.

Do not be discouraged when you realize that you can't ski on certain days. Give up and move on. You're going on a 6-day break however, even the top skiers will have off days. They typically pack up and head back to their homes to read a great book. Whatever you decide to do, do not muddle for a while hoping that you'll get better. It is possible to be able to recover however, more often than not, you won't and you may easily cause the type of damaging to confidence we're striving to stay clear of. Be aware of your limits.

FALLING

It's a difficult task to define the point at which a fall ceases to be it is a fall and turns into an accident. At the point you begin thinking about what to do to a crash, it is clear that you're actually flying. There is something you can do but that is to just relax as travel. If I refer to relaxation, I actually refer to Reeeelax with the capital letter R. It is the same for smaller falls, of course. If you Reeeelax and you are amazed what little harm you suffer even after a stunning wipeout.

You must forget the 'How-did-you-do-today?-Wow-I-didn't-fall-once' syndrome. If you want to be a better skier by pushing yourself to the limit, you'll fall. It's not like Alberto Tomba or Franz Klammer achieved their feats without a few accidents do you? You are, in fact, listening to some of the world's most renowned expert on crashes, and I'm still here. (See Chapter 1A, Release Bindings)

There's a second thing to keep in mind about falling that could help you reduce the fear. With reason, you'll notice that the higher the slope is and the lower your risk of harm yourself when you fall to the ground. It's not my intention to suggest that you try climbing this Couloir straight, or the Devil's Couloir right, but generally the falls that cause injury the most are those that fall that are on flat terrain. This is due to gravity and mass. There is a tendency to slide in a steep slope and then slowly come to a end, but on a flat surface like this you'll be able to Splat and end up in the middle of a wreck on the ground.

It follows that if you're going to fall often it is also likely be injured at least a couple of times. It could be anything from a thumb injury to a broken neck with knee ligaments pulled (being the most commonly injured) or anything in between. You might be surprised to learn that a study of ski-related accidents, conducted by an insurance company in France. French medical insurance firm, revealed that just 7 percent of the injuries reported within the French Alps in the course of the season included broken legs. It also showed that just 0.3 percent of skiers suffered an injury that was reported. When people say they're afraid to ski in the event of breaking the leg, we can observe that their odds of sustaining a fracture are around 5 times as likely against. This assumes you don't you aren't trying to fracture your leg or other parts equally important when you crank up your bindings to the maximum extent they can be, jumping off a cliff which proves to be higher than you anticipated or falling headlong into a pylon for a ski lift. These are fun skis, but they can also increase the chance of getting injured.

Therefore, we can conclude the fact that injuries with serious consequences are rare and far between. However, it is important to recognize that skiing is an activity that requires contact. In contrast to the numerous football matches, the majority of the contact will occur on the ground, however it is also rough and tough. If you've been raised with these kinds of games, you'll be able to accept the fact that injuries are inevitable, and is accepted in skiing. It is difficult to reconcile this reality in the face of the obvious paradox that skiing is a form of gentle therapy for relaxation. Every physical activity that is hard to perform tends to make you feel relaxed However, contacts sports are not designed to be gentle to the body. Alpine skiing was first invented in the early 20th century by university students who could jog themselves between three thousand vertical meters of mountain every day on deep snow. They weren't worried getting injured and had a great fitness level however, they were among the first people to ski on holidays.

Fitness is an essential aspect. It is not just a way for you to ski safely and safely, but it also helps prevent injuries and decreases the fear. If you're healthy the muscles and brain will be more responsive as well as your joints and ligaments will be more flexible and you'll feel great. If you're not fit at the beginning, you're putting your head down by putting a ball and chain around your neck and your head inside the paper bag. It's not going to be possible to complete the task in a timely manner and will soon feel less confident and be scared. I've discussed fitness as a positive factor in the past, but I believe that insufficiency is one of the major factors that cause fear, so if would like to become an improved skier, take off your old skis and start working. Being fit can cause an amount of discomfort and eventually, you recognize that your body can go through twists and turns you didn't believe were could be possible. If you decide to take on skis you'll be able to handle the pounding and tearing that can be dealt with much better. If you do your ski-training exercises done correctly you will be able to be able to ski the entire first day without having any adverse results, however, like everything else in the cruel world it is necessary to invest a lot of effort before you start.

DANGEROUS ACCESSORIES

"An unprofessional worker always takes responsibility for his tool', goes the saying, however I've always observed that a person who isn't a good worker however sloppy he might be, isn't able to tell whether the tools he uses can do the task or not. Most of the time, the tools are causing him to make a mistake at all times instead of the reverse being true. If your boots aren't tight in the heels, then you are able to move your feet as far as you'd like however the initial motion of your foot will not be transmitted through your boot , putting the skis on the edge. When the sides of your skis are rough and worn the skis won't be able to grip the turns and may not even move properly. It is possible that you are thinking that having a small number of holes made into the bottom of each ski will reduce your speed nicely and be grateful to the Lord for his small mercies, but have you tried to ski using a massive cut in one of your skis? It's as if there's something rotten stuck in the bottom of your shoe and it's impossible to remove it. It is essential to understand how your equipment works and what you can do to keep it in good condition.

SKI SCHOOL

Does this sound right? Doesn't the ski school's purpose teach us to ski? How could it be an influence that is negative?

It's the case that when you ski, there should be some kind of instruction process however, there could be many issues in a ski school. The system, which initially sets out to aid and motivate but can end up limiting the people who would like to use it.

Of course, I'm merely speculating, and I would like to say, prior to the time that I'm snubbed at the end of the ski pole, that I have met several outstanding instructors, whose teaching methods are a testament for the school system if the system were not overloaded with such technical rigor and an unshakeable conviction in its own worthiness. It is clear that the ski schools has taken on the light bulb phenomenon. Create an ideal light bulb and the companies would soon have to shut down. Create a system of instruction that is efficient that would allow the majority of novices to just require one week, at most and a few coaching session in the morning every holiday. The reality is that the student is faced with an abysmal mix of contradicting instruction given by different teachers who don't have the same level of proficiency that their class. Beautifully executed moves are displayed by an exemplary, but inarticulate, bronzed Adonis who's really just in the resort to get some points in his belt. It's not surprising to meet those who've been at and away from the ski school throughout their lives as hardened feline burglars who have been through prison and out.

The ski school has to be in existence, and its primary goal should be to demonstrate to its students how to learn. The learning process itself must be followed by the student independently, racking miles and setting himself achievable tasks. Of course, the ski school provides other services like kindergartens and guiding, but it is the teaching methods that are the issue in this article. If you discover yourself as a student that you don't understand a lesson or find it difficult to follow or get your teacher to demonstrate the way, you need to consider: Is this helping? Do I have a better understanding? Do I have a waste of money? Do I need to buy a copy of Better Skiing What do you think?

It's simple to me to state "caveat emptor," however, how can a purchaser be safe if he's not aware of the potential pitfalls? Beginners will be unable to do this however, it's much easier for novices as well as advanced skiers when they find an instructor who is reliable. It is wise to look for advice from an impartial source who knows how to locate the most effective instructor, or even the most reputable skiing school or the most suitable resort to meet your needs.

I've thought for a while that time that instruction in skiing should be based on theoretical concepts that could be discussed at after a long day of skiing in a cozy cabin at the bottom of the mountain, with the gluwein in a big mug! The instructor will make an ice skate and a boot and explains what they're all about and how they operate. Maybe he will also tell you about the different types of snow, the best way to avoid avalanches, the other skiers, and anything else that isn't easily discussed on the mountain. Each student is a part of any weekly ski class and will give them a sense of the surroundings they were in and things they skied on.

POSTING A BEGINNER ON THE REAR TRACK

I've often heard individuals trying to instruct their wives and friends and wives, and their relatives, to ski with no clue what they were discussing. I did not. It was obvious that the child didn't I'm curious as to how many of them were able to turn into skiers or quit.

Sometimes, due to frustration with your system, or perhaps because romance might be at hand and you are the best skier, may feel the desire to coach beginners yourself. While I don't recommend this as always the best option however I am unable to suggest against it. In the end when you've read this book, you'll become an expert, won't you? It's also a good idea to review a few fundamental rules if you're planning to instruct someone on how to ski or to give them advice.

Keep in mind that a newbie is almost always in a state of shock. He'll be able to learn very little the way of technical jargon and all information will have to be demonstrated. Even placing his skis and boots on is a challenge.

Reduce your vocabulary at a minimal, and make it easy. Create a list of terms to illustrate the proper way to do it. Always encourage. Always tell them "Do this in this manner'. Never mention: 'Don't do that'. Don't do this.' It's too complicated.

Always use positive words. If needed, point out an error through demonstration, followed by an explanation of the issue and what the student is doing incorrectly, then proceed to the proper method. Repeat the movements and overdo the movements if needed. Be patient. Make the exercises easy for your student and then make it easier for him to master the task slowly. Be aware of his needs and take your time thinking about how you intend to present something before beginning to describe the subject. Make sure you remember what you felt when you were just beginning and how you'd like it be said. Don't forget, if you aren't interested in teaching or don't think that you are capable of it, stop teaching!

You might be thinking about why this book has turned into a ski instructor's guide, but unless you want to resist the lure of sharing your knowledge to someone who doesn't, you may be well aware of the risks. Referring back to what I wrote in the first section, I've been given instructions by amateur instructors who a rubber-limbed instructor would struggle with. For example, bending the lower shoulder to an angle towards the front of the ski' Point the upper ski downwards and lean back! could seriously hamper the progression of a beginner.

If you are able to see why these directions will not work maybe you can be able to become an excellent teacher! Finding out how you can describe a move to someone who isn't you isn't a bad idea to do, as it can assist you in be aware of what you're doing, and encourage your mind to focus while performing it! Be wary of performing it at your friend's cost.

MOTORIZATION, HOLIDAYS, AND MONEY

How long your trip can affect your progress so the further you go skiing, the more efficient you'll be. Since most skiers only go skiing for a week it is not enough time to develop your rhythm. It's all about what you think of skiing; the most skilled skiers on the mountain in addition to the natives, are those who are able to do it for about two or three months during winter. They're either wealthy and have the money to afford it or have invested everything in skiing and then tossed everything else aside, with the exception of the two-tone old VW camper.

However, it is possible that, if you're extremely motivated, you could be in peak skiing condition as soon as you put on your skis. It might take just around an hour to regain your confidence. To achieve this, you'll need to have spent at least two months working out on your own fitness program however it is doable!

Conclusion

We thank you for purchasing this book. We are sincerely hoping that we've provided you with some tips to use in the event that you decide to take the first time you take a skydive. Many people consider skydiving as "nothing" thinking that it is of no economic value, and is even thought of as unproductive in terms of time and energy. It's not going to solve the problem of world hunger or bring peace to the world. However, as many skydivers have said that skydiving is everything? It's fun, and friendship and risk and joy and peace, and even the possibility of death as well.

www.ingramcontent.com/pod-product-compliance
Lightning Source LLC
Chambersburg PA
CBHW050400120526
44590CB00015B/1759